MINUTE
GUIDE TO
Word
FOR WINDOWS 6

Peter Aitken

alpha books

A Division of Prentice Hall Computer Publishing

201 W. 103rd Street, Indianapolis, Indiana 46290 USA

©1993 by Alpha Books

International Standard Book Number: 1-56761-345-4
Library of Congress Catalog Card Number: 93-72389

95 94   8 7 6 5 4

Interpretation of the printing code: the rightmost number of the first series of numbers is the year of the book's printing; the rightmost number of the second series of numbers is the number of the book's printing. For example, a printing code of 93-1 shows that the first printing of the book occurred in 1993.

Screen reproductions in this book were created by means of the program Collage Plus from Inner Media, Inc., Hollis, NH.

Special thanks to C. Herbert Feltner for ensuring the technical accuracy of this book.

Printed in the United States of America

Publisher: Marie Butler-Knight
Associate Publisher: Lisa Bucki
Managing Editor: Elizabeth Keaffaber
Acquisitions Manager: Stephen R. Poland
Development Editor: Mary Cole Rack
Production Editor/Manuscript Editor: Audra Gable
Book Designer: Roger Morgan
Cover Design: Dan Armstrong
Indexer: Craig Alan Small
Production: Diana Bigham, Katy Bodenmiller, Brad Chinn, Scott Cook, Tim Cox, Meshell Dinn, Terri Edwards, Mark Enochs, Howard Jones, Beth Rago, Marc Shecter, Greg Simsic

Contents

Trademarks

All terms mentioned in this book that are known to be trademarks or service marks are listed below. In addition, terms that are suspected of being trademarks or service marks have been capitalized. Alpha Books cannot attest to the accuracy of this information. Use of a term in this book should not be regarded as affecting the validity of any trademark or service mark.

1-2-3 is a registered trademark of Lotus Development Corporation.

AutoCAD is a registered trademark of Autodesk Inc.

Micrografx is a registered trademark of Micrografx Inc.

Windows and Toolbar are trademarks of Microsoft Corporation.

Introduction

Microsoft Word has long been considered the premier word processing program for the Windows operating environment. And now, with the release of version 6.0, the program is even better. In a single package you have everything you need to create anything from a one-page memo to a polished 500-page report.

It's unavoidable that a program with so much power be somewhat complex. Learning all of its features can take some time—time that you can't spare from your busy schedule. You need a fast method of learning the program's most important features. You want to get up and running quickly so that you can start using Word productively in your day-to-day tasks.

Welcome to the *10 Minute Guide to Word for Windows*. I believe that this book is exactly what you are looking for. It teaches you the basics of Word in a series of short lessons, each of which can be completed in 10 minutes or less. Each lesson is self-contained, allowing you to start and stop as your schedule allows. The features of the *10 Minute Guide to Word for Windows* make it ideal for anyone who

- Has limited time available for learning the program.

- Is intimidated by the complexity of Word for Windows.

- Needs a clear and concise guide to the program's most important features.

- Just upgraded from the previous version and needs a quick guide to changes in the program.

What Is the 10 Minute Guide?

The 10 Minute Guide series is a new approach to computer books. Instead of trying to cover every detail of a program, the 10 Minute Guide concentrates on those features that are essential for most users—those features that you need to get your work done! Concepts and operations are explained in plain English, so you won't have to wade through technical jargon and computerese!

Conventions Used in this Book

Throughout the book the following icons are used to help you find information more quickly:

Plain English   New or unfamiliar terms are explained for you in straightforward, everyday language.

Timesaver Tip   These tips offer hints and shortcuts to help you use the program efficiently.

Panic Button   This icon warns you of potential problems and offers practical solutions.

In addition, the following conventions are used to organize the book's material:

1.	Numbered steps provide exact instructions for frequently needed procedures.
`On-screen text`	Messages that appear on-screen are displayed in a special computer font.
What you type	Text that you enter will appear in bold, color computer font.

Items you select	Commands, options, and icons you select or keys you press will appear in color.
Selection letters	Boldface letters within a menu title, menu option, or dialog box option indicate selection letters for keyboard shortcuts. These correspond to the underlined letters on-screen.
Key combinations	In many cases, you are instructed to press a two-key combination in order to enter a command. When the text says "press Alt+X," it means to hold down the Alt key and press X. Then release both keys.

Using This Book

On the inside front cover of the book you'll find concise instructions for installing Word for Windows on your system. The inside back cover features a guide to the Standard toolbar buttons.

This book contains 28 lessons. I suggest that you work through them in order. After reading the first seven lessons, however, you can jump around to find specific information quickly. Once you have read all the lessons you will have a good grounding in the most important features of the Word for Windows program. If you want to go further and explore the program's many advanced features, I recommend the *Word for Windows HyperGuide*.

Lesson

Getting Started

In this lesson, you'll start Word for Windows, learn the parts of the Word for Windows screen, and learn how to quit the program. You'll also learn about the Standard toolbar.

Starting Word for Windows

To start Word for Windows, it must be installed on your system. See the inside front cover of this book for default installation instructions, or follow the instructions provided in the Word for Windows package. After you install Word for Windows, your Windows Program Manager screen will include a Word for Windows 6.0 window, and that window will contain a Microsoft Word 6.0 icon. To start the program, double-click the icon. If you're unsure about this procedure, or about using the mouse, please refer to the appendix, "Microsoft Windows Primer."

What's an Icon?   An *icon* is a small graphic symbol that Windows uses to represent a program or screen window.

The Waiting Game   While the mouse pointer appears as an hourglass on-screen, you must wait.

Parts of the Screen

When you start Word for Windows, it displays its opening logo for a few seconds and then displays its main screen with a blank document that's ready for your input. Depending on how your system is set up, it may also display a Tip of the Day box containing a brief, useful tip about the Word for Windows program. Press Enter to hide the Tip box.

Tip of the Day   You can learn a lot from this small window in Word's opening screen, but if it becomes a nuisance just turn it off by clicking the Show Tips at Startup box. If you change your mind later, select Tip of the Day from the Help menu.

Take a moment to familiarize yourself with the Word for Windows screen. It contains a number of useful components, which are labeled in Figure 1.1.

- The *title bar* displays the program name and the name of the document being edited.

- The *menu bar* contains the main Word for Windows menu.

- The *Standard toolbar* displays buttons that you can select to perform commonly needed editing tasks. You must have a mouse to use the toolbar.

- The *Formatting toolbar* is used to select character and paragraph formatting commands. It, too, is accessed only with the mouse.

- The *Ruler* controls margins, indents, and tab stops.

- The *work area* is where your document is displayed.

- The *scroll bars* are used to move around your document with the mouse.

- The *status line* displays information about your document.

Menu bar   Title bar   Standard toolbar

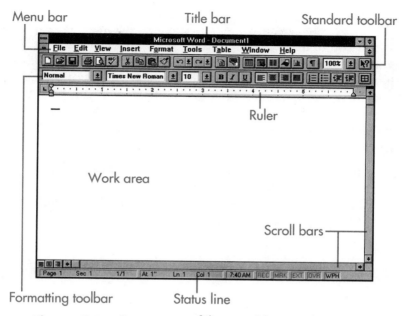

Ruler

Work area

Scroll bars

Formatting toolbar   Status line

Figure 1.1 Components of the Word for Windows screen.

The Standard Toolbar

The Standard toolbar contains buttons that you select with the mouse to perform commonly needed tasks. For example, the far left button represents the File New command, and the button next to it represents the File Open command. If you position the mouse pointer on a toolbar button (without clicking), the status bar will display a brief description of the button's function.

You'll probably find that clicking on a toolbar button is quicker and more convenient than entering the entire command sequence. The inside back cover of this book lists the Standard toolbar buttons and their functions.

Quitting Word for Windows

When you're done using Word for Windows, quit the program by pressing Alt+F4 or by selecting File Exit. With the
mouse, position the pointer on the box to the left of the title
bar (the Control-menu box) and double-click. If you have any
unsaved documents, Word for Windows prompts you to save
them. Then the program terminates, and you're returned to
the Program Manager screen.

In this lesson you learned how to start Word for Win-
dows, the parts of the screen, and how to quit Word for
Windows. In the next lesson you'll learn how to use the
Word for Windows Help system.

Lesson

The Help System

In this lesson, you'll learn how to use the Word for Windows on-line help system.

The Help Command

One way to access the help system is via the **Help** command on the main menu. As you can see in Figure 2.1, the **Help** pull-down menu has nine commands.

Figure 2.1 The Help menu.

- Contents displays the main Help table of contents.

- Search for Help on lets you search through Help for information relating to a specific keyword.

- Index calls up the main help system index.

- Quick Preview lists introductory lessons for getting started with Word.

- Examples and Demos lists the lessons available in the Word tutorial.

- **Tip** of the Day displays a brief, helpful tip about the Word for Windows program.

- **WordPerfect Help** displays help for users of the WordPerfect word processing program.

- **Technical Support** displays information about support that is available for Microsoft Word.

- **About Microsoft Word** lists information about the Word for Windows program, such as the program version number and the license number.

The most often used **Help** commands are explained in the following sections. Refer to your program documentation if you would like detailed information on the Word for Windows tutorials and the WordPerfect Help command.

The Help Index

The **Help Index** is command central for the help system. Using the index, you can easily locate help information on any topic. To display the opening page of the index, select Help Index or press F1 while working in your document (as opposed to while you're using the menus or a dialog box). The Help window is displayed initially as a smaller window overlapping part of your document screen, as shown in Figure 2.2.

Just Like Any Other Window Remember that the Help window is like any other window. You can move it, resize it, or close it using the usual techniques.

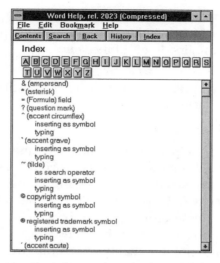

Figure 2.2 The Help window displaying the Help Index.

Using the Index

The Help window has five buttons at the top. Use these buttons to move around the help system. To select a button, click on it with the mouse or press Alt+n, where *n* is the underlined character in the button name. Remember that if a button appears gray, the corresponding option is not currently available.

- Contents displays the Help Contents.

- History lets you select from a list of the Help topics you viewed recently.

- Back displays the last Help topic you viewed.

- Search displays a screen from which you can search for the topic of interest.

- Index displays the letters of the alphabet as buttons across the Help window. For information on a topic, click on the first letter of its name.

Where Is It?   Use the Help Index to find the topic of interest.

Within the help system certain terms and phrases are underlined and displayed in a different color. A solid underline denotes a cross-reference. Selecting a cross-reference takes you directly to help information on that topic. A dotted underline denotes a term or phrase for which a definition is available. When you position the mouse on an underlined term, the mouse pointer changes to a pointing hand. You can use the keyboard to move a highlight bar between underlined terms by pressing Tab or Shift+Tab.

- To jump to a cross-reference, click on the term or highlight it and press Enter.

- To display a definition, point at it and press the left mouse button, or highlight it and press Enter. The definition will be displayed in a pop-up box until you click the mouse button or press Enter again.

Context-Sensitive Help

The Word for Windows help system is context-sensitive. This means that if you are selecting a menu command or entering information in a dialog box, pressing F1 will automatically display help information on your current task. Once the Help window is displayed, you can use all of its features to access additional information. When you close the Help window, you are returned to your task right where you left off.

In this lesson, you learned how to use the Word for Windows help system. In the next lesson, you'll learn how to create a new document.

Lesson

Creating a
New Document

In this lesson, you'll learn how to create a new document, how to move around the screen, and how to select text.

Entering Text

When you start Word for Windows, after hiding the Tip of the Day, you see a blank work area that contains only two items:

- The blinking vertical line marks the insertion point, the location where text you type will be inserted into the document and where certain editing actions will occur.

- The horizontal line is the end-of-document marker.

Since your new document is empty, these two markers are at the same location. To enter text, simply type on the keyboard. As you type, the text is inserted, and the insertion point moves to the right. If the line reaches the right edge of the screen, Word for Windows automatically moves to the start of the next line; this is called *wrapping*. Press Enter only when you want to start a new paragraph. As you enter more lines than will fit on the screen, Word for Windows automatically scrolls previously entered text upward to keep the insertion point in view.

Leave It to Word Wrap   Press Enter only when you want to start a new paragraph.

Moving Around the Screen

As you work on a document, you will often have to move the insertion point so that you can view or work on other regions of text. Table 3.1 shows you how to move the insertion point using the mouse or the keyboard.

Table 3.1   Moving the Insertion Point Around the Screen

To move here	Perform this action
With the mouse	
Up or down one line	Click on the up or down arrow on the vertical scroll bar.
Up or down one screen	Click on the vertical scroll bar between the box and the up or down arrow.
Up or down any amount	Drag the scroll bar box up or down.
To any visible location	Click on the location.
With the keyboard	
Left or right one character	Press ← or →.
Up or down one line	Press ↑ or ↓.
Left or right one word	Press Ctrl+← or Ctrl+→.
Up or down one paragraph	Press Ctrl+↑ or Ctrl+↓.
Start or end of a line	Press Home or End.
Up or down one screen	Press PgUp or PgDn.

| Top or bottom of screen | Press Ctrl+PgUp or Ctrl+PgDn. |
| Start or end of the document | Press Ctrl+Home or Ctrl+End. |

Selecting Text

Many Word for Windows operations require that you first select the text to be modified. For example, to change a word to italics, you must select the word first and then specify italics. Selected text is displayed on the screen in reverse video, as shown in Figure 3.1, which has the phrase Dear Mr. Johnson selected.

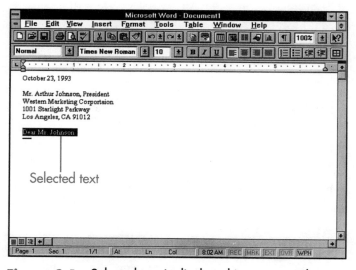

Figure 3.1   Selected text is displayed in reverse video.

You can select text with either the mouse or the key-board. With the mouse, you can use the *selection bar,* an unmarked column in the left document margin. When the mouse pointer moves from the document to the selection bar, it changes from an I-beam to an arrow. Table 3.2 gives the methods for selecting text with the mouse or the keyboard.

Table 3.2   Methods of Selecting Text

To select	Perform this action
With the mouse	
Any amount	Point at the start of the text and drag the highlight over the text.
One word	Double-click anywhere on the word.
One sentence	Press and hold Ctrl and click anywhere in the sentence.
One line	Click on the selection bar next to the line.
Multiple lines	Drag in the selection bar next to the lines.
One paragraph	Double-click on the selection bar next to the paragraph.
Entire document	Press and hold Ctrl and click anywhere in the selection bar.
With the keyboard	
Any amount	Move the insertion point to the start of the text, press and hold Shift, and move the insertion point to the end of the desired text using the movement keys described in Table 3.1.
Entire document	Press Ctrl+5 (the numeric keypad 5).

To cancel a selection, click anywhere on the screen or use the keyboard to move the insertion point.

Fast Selection   Double-click on a word to select it.

Deleting Text

You can delete single characters or larger blocks of text.

- To delete the character to the right of the insertion point, press Del.

- To delete the character to the left of the insertion point, press Backspace.

- To delete a block of text, select the text and then press Del or Backspace.

If you make a mistake when deleting, you can recover deleted text with the Edit Undo command. This command appears on the Edit menu as either Undo Typing or Undo Clear, depending on how you deleted the text. In either case, the effect is the same: the deleted characters are replaced in their original position. You must select this command immediately after deleting and before performing any other action. You can also click on the Undo button on the Standard toolbar or press the shortcut key Ctrl+Z to undo the deletion.

In this lesson, you learned how to enter, select, and delete text. In the next lesson, you'll learn how to control the way Word displays documents on your screen.

Lesson

Controlling the Screen Display

In this lesson, you'll learn how to control the Word for Windows screen display to suit your working style.

Document Display Modes

Word for Windows offers four different modes in which you can display your document.

Normal Mode

Most often you'll probably want to work in Normal mode. This is Word for Windows' default display. Figure 4.1 shows a document in Normal mode. As you can see, all special formatting is visible on-screen. Different font sizes, italics, boldface, and other enhancements are displayed on the screen very much as they will appear on the printed page. Certain aspects of the page layout, however, are simplified in order to speed editing. For example, headers and footers are not displayed. Normal mode is fine for most editing tasks.

Select View Normal to switch to Normal view. In the View menu, the currently selected mode has a dot displayed next to it.

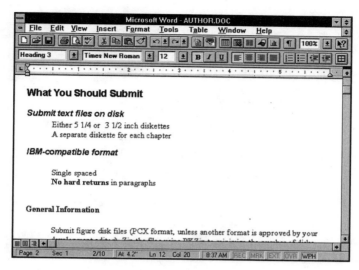

Figure 4.1 A document displayed in Normal mode.

Outline Mode

Use **Outline** mode to create outlines and to examine the structure of a document. Figure 4.2 shows the sample document in Outline mode. Here you can choose to view your document headings only, hiding all subordinate text. Document headings, along with subordinate text, can be quickly promoted, demoted, or moved to a new location. In order for this to be of much use, you need to assign heading styles to the document headings, a technique you'll learn more about in Lesson 20.

Select View Outline to switch to Outline view.

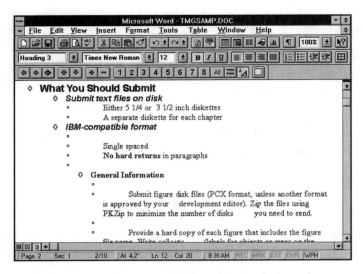

Figure 4.2   A document displayed in Outline mode.

Page Layout Mode

Page Layout mode displays your document exactly as it will be printed. Headers, footers, and all the details of page layout are displayed on-screen. You can perform editing in **Page** Layout mode, and in fact this mode is ideal when you are fine-tuning the details of page composition. Be aware, however, that the additional computer processing that's required makes display changes relatively slow in **Page** Layout mode, particularly when you have a complex page layout. Figure 4.3 shows the sample document in **Page** Layout mode.

Select View Page Layout to switch to **Page** Layout view.

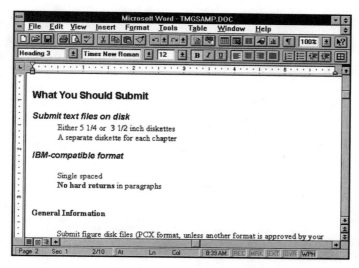

Figure 4.3   A document displayed in Page Layout mode.

View It First!   Use **P**age Layout mode to see what your document will look like when it is printed.

Draft Font Mode

Draft Font mode is a display option that can be applied in both Normal and Outline views. As Figure 4.4 illustrates, a single generic font is used for screen display, and special formatting such as italics and boldface are indicated by underlining. Draft Font mode provides the fastest editing and screen display, and is ideal when you are concentrating on the contents of your document more than on its appearance.

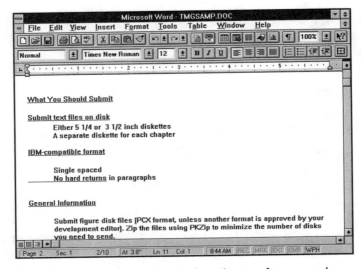

Figure 4.4   A document displayed in Draft Font mode.

To turn Draft Font mode on or off:

1.   Select Tools Options to display the Options dialog box.

2.   If necessary, click the View tab to display the View options.

3.   Select the Draft Font option to turn it on or off.

4.   Select OK.

Full Screen Display

To see the maximum amount of text on the screen, select View Full Screen. In Full Screen mode, the title bar, menu, toolbars, status line, and all other Word elements are hidden, and the full screen is devoted to text. You can enter and edit text in this mode, and can select from the menus using the usual keyboard commands. To turn off Full Screen mode, select View Full Screen again or click the Full icon that is displayed in the lower right corner of the screen.

Ruler and Toolbar Display

The Word for Windows default is to display the Ruler, Standard toolbar, and Formatting toolbar at the top of the editing screen. At times, however, you may want to hide one or more of these items to give yourself a larger work area and a less cluttered screen. Of course, you will not have access to the editing features of the item(s) you have hidden.

To control the screen display of the Ruler, select View to display the View menu, and then select Ruler to toggle the Ruler display between on and off. To control the toolbars, select View Toolbars to display the Toolbars dialog box. Turn the Standard and Formatting options on or off as desired, and then select OK.

The Whole Picture   Hide the Ruler and toolbars when you need to display the maximum amount of text but don't want to use Full Screen mode.

Zooming the Screen

The View Zoom command lets you control the size of your document as displayed on the screen. You can enlarge the size to facilitate reading small fonts, or decrease the size to view an entire page at one time. When you select View Zoom, the dialog box in Figure 4.5 is displayed.

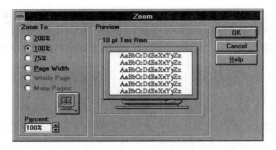

Figure 4.5   The Zoom dialog box.

In this dialog box, you have the following options. As you make selections the Preview section of the dialog box shows you what the selected zoom setting will look like.

- Under Zoom To, select the desired page magnification. 200% is twice normal size, 75% is three-quarters normal size, etc. In the Percent box you can enter a custom magnification in the range 10–200%.

- Select Page Width to have Word for Windows automatically scale the display to fit the entire page width on the screen.

- Select Whole Page to have Word for Windows automatically scale the display to fit the entire page on the screen.

- Select Many Pages to display two or more pages at the same time. Click the monitor button under the Many Pages option then drag to specify how many pages to display.

Note that the Whole Page and Many Pages options are available only if you are viewing the document in Page Layout mode.

In this lesson, you learned how to control the Word for Windows screen display. In the next lesson, you'll learn how to save documents.

Lesson

Saving Documents

5

In this lesson, you'll learn how to name your document, save it to disk, and enter summary information.

Saving a Document for the First Time

When you create a new document in Word for Windows, it is stored temporarily in your computer's memory under the default name Document*n*, where *n* is a number that increases by one for each new unnamed document. The document is only "remembered" until you quit the program or the computer is turned off. To save a document permanently so you can retrieve it later, you must save it to disk. This is done with the File Save command, or by selecting the File Save button on the Standard toolbar.

When you save a document for the first time, you must assign it another name. When you select File Save for an unnamed document (or File Save As for any document), Word for Windows displays the Save As dialog box, as shown in Figure 5.1.

In the File Name text box, enter the name you want to assign to the document file. The name can be 1 to 8 characters long, and should be descriptive of the document's contents. Then select OK. Word for Windows automatically adds the .DOC extension when the file is saved.

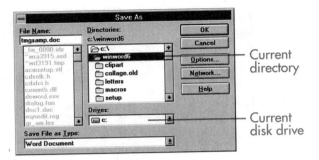

Figure 5.1 The Save As dialog box.

What's an Extension? The extension is the 1- to 3-letter part of a file name to the right of the period.

What happens next depends on the setting of the Prompt for Summary Info option. To set this option, select Tools Options, click the Save tab, and then select the Prompt for Summary Info box. If the option is turned off, Word immediately saves your document. If the option is turned on, Word displays the Summary Info dialog box, which is shown in Figure 5.2. This figure shows typical summary information that you might want to use. You can ignore this dialog box, or you can enter information here that will later be useful in keeping track of your documents.

- Title: Enter the title of the document. This is not the same as the document's file name.

- Subject: Enter a phrase describing the subject of the document.

- Author: Word automatically fills this field with the user name you entered when installing the program. You can change it if you like.

- Keywords: Enter one or more words related to the document's contents.

- Comments: Enter any information you want saved with the document.

- Statistics: Click on the Statistics button to display information about the document, such as the number of words, last date edited, and so on.

Figure 5.2 The Summary Info dialog box.

Summary Info Box Doesn't Appear? Select Summary Info from the File menu to display it.

Viewing Statistics At any time, select File Summary Info Statistics to view a document's statistics.

After entering any summary information, click on OK. Word for Windows saves the document, along with the summary information you entered, in a file with the name you specified. You are then returned to the document screen, with the newly assigned file name displayed in the title bar.

Saving a Named Document

As you work on a document, you should save it now and then to minimize possible data loss in the event of a power failure or other system problem. Once you have assigned a name to a document, the File Save command saves the current document version under its assigned name; no dialog boxes are displayed.

Don't Forget! Save your document regularly as you work on it.

Changing a Document Name

You may wish to save a named document under a new name. For example, you might want to keep the old version under the original name and the revised version under a new name. To change a document name, select File Save As. The Save As dialog box is displayed, showing the current document name in the File Name text box. Then take the following steps:

1. Change the file name to the desired new name.

2. (Optional) Select a directory in the Directories list box to save the document in a different directory.

3. (Optional) Select a drive from the Drives drop-down box to save the document on a different disk drive.

4. Select OK. The document is saved under the new name.

Changing Summary Information

You can change the summary information associated with a document at any time. Select File Summary Info, and the Summary Info dialog box will be displayed. Make the desired changes and select OK. The new information will be registered with the document the next time you save the file.

In this lesson, you learned how to save a document, change a document name, and enter document summary information. In the next lesson, you'll learn how to retrieve a document from disk.

Lesson

Retrieving Documents

In this lesson, you'll learn how to retrieve a document from disk into Word for Windows, how to search for a specific file, and how to import documents that were created with other programs.

Retrieving a Document This means to reopen a document from your disk into Word for Windows so you can work on it.

Retrieving a Word for Windows Document

You can retrieve any document created with Word for Windows for further editing, printing, and so on. To do so, select File Open or click on the File Open button on the Standard toolbar. The Open dialog box will be displayed, as shown in Figure 6.1.

Opening a Document Use File **O**pen to work on a document that you saved earlier.

In the File Name text box, the current file template is listed. By default this is *.doc, meaning that the dialog box will list all files with the .DOC extension (the default extension for Word for Windows files). The File Name list box lists all files in the current directory that match that description.

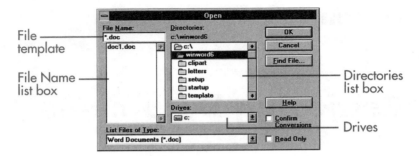

Figure 6.1 The Open dialog box.

> **File Template** A *file template* tells Word for Windows the types of file names to list according to their file name extensions.

- To retrieve a file, type its name in the File Name text box, and press Enter. Or, you can double-click on its name in the File Name list box. The file will be read from disk and displayed for editing.

- To retrieve a file from a different directory, select the desired directory from the Directories list box.

- To retrieve a file from a different disk, select the desired disk from the Drives drop-down box.

- To open a file in read-only mode, select the Read Only check box before retrieving the file. If you modify a read-only file, you can save it only under a new name using the File Save As command; you cannot save modifications under the existing name.

Finding a File

If you cannot remember the full name or location of the file that you want to retrieve, use the Find File button in the Open dialog box to find it by name, contents, and/or summary information. When you select Find File, Word for Windows displays the Search dialog box, shown in Figure 6.2. Make entries in this dialog box as described in these steps:

1. Pull down the File Name list to select the type of file to search for, or enter your own template in the File Name text box. For example, to find all Word documents whose names start with C, enter the template C*.DOC.

2. Pull down the Location list to specify the disk to be searched, or type in the path of the subdirectory to search.

3. (Optional) Check the Rebuild File List check box if you want the file list resulting from your search to replace the list from an earlier search.

4. (Optional) Check the Include Subdirectories check box if you want Word to search subdirectories.

5. (Optional) Select Advanced Search, and then make selections in the dialog box to have Word base the search on the file's summary information or its time and date of creation.

Figure 6.2   The Search dialog box.

6.   Once the dialog box entries are complete, select OK. Word searches the specified disk/directory and displays the Find File dialog box shown in Figure 6.3.

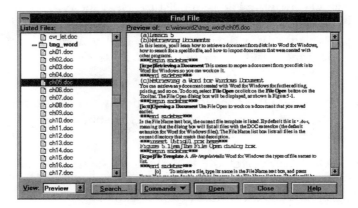

Figure 6.3   The Find File dialog box.

The Find File dialog box is split into these two areas:

- The Listed Files box lists the names of all the matching files, sorted by subdirectory and name. You can scroll through this list using the keyboard or the mouse.

- The Preview of box displays the contents of the highlighted file. When the Preview of box is active you can scroll using the keyboard or mouse to view more of the file's contents.

The View pull-down list in the lower left corner lets you control what's displayed in the Preview of section. You can display the highlighted file's summary information, or a more detailed file list, instead of a preview of the file's contents.

The buttons at the bottom of the Find File dialog box offer the following options:

- Select **Open** to retrieve the highlighted file into Word.

- Select **Search** to start another search.

- Select **Close** to close the dialog box and return to Word.

- Select **Commands** for a list of other actions from which you can choose: Open Read Only, Print, Summary, Delete, Copy, and Sorting.

Memory Helper Use the Find File window to locate a file whose name you've forgotten.

Importing Documents

You can import documents that were created with other applications, converting them to Word for Windows format. For example, you could import a document that was created with WordPerfect 5.1, retaining all of its special formatting and fonts. Word for Windows can import from a wide variety of programs. To import a file, follow these steps:

1. Select File Open or click on the File Open button on the Standard toolbar. The Open dialog box will be displayed.

2. (Optional) Open the List Files of Type drop-down box. Select the type of file you want to import.

3. (Optional) Select the Confirm Conversions check box.

4. The File Name list box lists all files of the type you specified in the List Files of Type box (with the indicated extension). Select the file to import, or type its name directly into the File Name box.

5. Select OK. If the Confirm Conversions option is checked, Word for Windows asks you to confirm the type of file being imported.

6. Select OK. The file is imported and converted to Word for Windows format.

In this lesson, you learned how to retrieve a document from disk into Word for Windows, how to search for a specific file, and how to import documents that were created with other programs. In the next lesson, you'll learn how to print your document.

Lesson

Printing Your Document

In this lesson, you'll learn how to print your document.

Quick Printing

To print a Word for Windows document, you must have installed and selected the printer you are going to use. The printer must be turned on and on-line. To print the entire document using the current settings:

1. Select File Print or press Ctrl+P. The Print dialog box is displayed (see Figure 7.1).

2. Select OK. The document is printed.

Speedy Printing   To print one copy of the entire document without going to the Print dialog box, click on the Print button on the Standard toolbar.

Printer Not Working?   Refer to your Microsoft Windows and printer documentation for help.

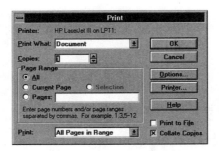

Figure 7.1   The Print dialog box.

Printing Part of a Document

You can print a single page of a document or a range of
pages. This can be useful for checking the results of your
formatting and other document components. To print
specific pages, follow these steps:

1. If you're printing a single page, position the inser-
    tion point anywhere on the page to be printed.

2. Select File Print or press Ctrl+P. The Print dialog
    box is displayed.

3. Under Page Range, select Current Page to print the
    page the insertion point is on. Select Pages to print
    a range of pages, and then enter the beginning and
    ending page numbers, separated by a dash, in the
    box (for example, 2–6). If you want to print specific
    noncontiguous pages, enter the page numbers
    separated by a comma (for example, 1,3).

4. Select OK. The selected page or pages are printed.

Setting Up the Page

By default, Word for Windows formats printer output for
8 1/2-by-11-inch paper in portrait orientation. You can

modify these settings if needed (if you want to print on 8 1/2-by-14-inch legal paper, for example).

> **Orientation**   Orientation refers to the way in which your text is printed on the page. Portrait orientation is the default and prints text parallel to the short edge of the paper. Landscape orientation prints text parallel to the long edge of the paper.

To change the print orientation or the paper size:

1.   Select File Page Setup. The Page Setup dialog box is displayed.

2.   Click the Paper Size tab.

3.   Select Paper Size to open the drop-down box. Word for Windows lists several common paper sizes.

4.   Select the desired paper size.

5.   If you select Custom Size, use the Height and Width boxes to specify the actual paper size.

6.   Under Orientation, select Portrait or Landscape.

7.   Select OK. The new settings will be in effect for your document and will be used the next time it is printed.

Previewing the Print Job

You can view a screen display that previews exactly what your document will look like when printed. To do so, follow these steps:

1.   Select File Print Preview. The current page is displayed in preview mode (see Figure 7.2).

One Page button

Multiple Pages button

Zoom Percent list

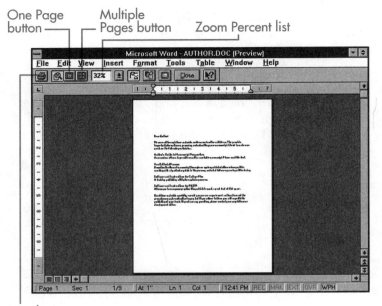

Print button

Figure 7.2 The Print Preview screen.

2. Press PgUp or PgDn or use the scroll bar to view other pages.

3. Click on the Multiple Pages button, and then drag over the page icons to preview more than one page at once. Click on the One Page button to preview a single page.

4. Pull down the Zoom Percent list and select a magnification to preview the document at different magnifications.

5. Click on the Print button to print the document.

6. Click on Close or press Esc to end Print Preview display.

Using Print Options

There are several printing options available that you may find useful. To use these options:

1. Select File Print or press Ctrl+P. The Print dialog box is displayed.

2. Select Options. The Options dialog box (shown in Figure 7.3) is displayed.

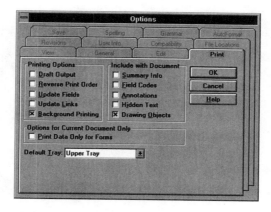

Figure 7.3   The Options dialog box.

3. Under Printing Options, select one or more of the following:

   • **Draft Output** produces draft output that prints faster but may lack some graphics and formatting (depending on your specific printer).

   • **Reverse Print Order** prints pages in last-to-first order. This setting produces collated output on printers that have face-up output.

   • **Update Fields** automatically updates all document fields (except locked ones) before printing.

4.   Select OK. You are returned to the Print dialog box.

5.   Select OK to begin printing.

In this lesson, you learned how to print all or part of your documents. In the next lesson, you'll learn how to move and copy text.

Lesson

Moving and Copying Text

In this lesson, you'll learn how to move and copy text in your document.

Selecting Text

In Lesson 3, you learned how to select a block of text in order to delete it. You use the same procedures to select text you want to move or copy. Remember, selected text is displayed on the screen in reverse video.

Copying Text

When you copy text, you place a duplicate of the selected text in a new location. After you copy, the text exists in both the original and new locations. There are several methods available for copying text.

> **Save Your Fingers** Copying text can save you typing. For example, copy a paragraph to a new location when you need to modify it slightly.

Using the Clipboard to Copy

The Clipboard is a temporary storage location offered in Windows programs. You can copy text from one location in your document to the Clipboard, and then paste it from the Clipboard to the new location in your document.

1. Select the text to be copied. The selected text is highlighted, as shown in Figure 8.1.

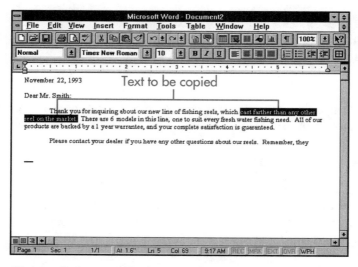

Figure 8.1 Highlighted text to be copied.

2. Select Edit Copy. Alternatively, you can click on the Copy button on the Standard toolbar or press Ctrl+C.

3. Move the insertion point to the new location for the text.

4. Select Edit Paste. You can also select the Paste button on the Standard toolbar or press Ctrl+V. The text is inserted at the new location, as shown in Figure 8.2.

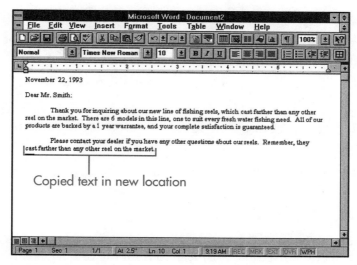

Figure 8.2 The copied text in the new location.

Again and Again You can paste the same text from the Clipboard more than once. The text remains there, throughout your work session, until it is replaced with new text.

Using the Mouse to Copy

A shortcut for copying is available if you're using the mouse:

1. Select the text to copy.

2. Using the mouse, point at the location where you want the text copied.

3. Press and hold Ctrl+Shift and click the right mouse button.

Copying Text That You Just Typed

You can quickly insert a copy of text that you just typed at a different document location:

1. At one document location, type the text to be copied.

2. Move the insertion point to the second location for the text.

3. Select Edit Repeat Typing or press F4.

Moving Text

Text can be moved from one document location to another. When you move text, it is *deleted* from the original location and inserted at the new location.

Moving Text with the Clipboard

You can move text with the Clipboard. These are the steps to follow:

1. Select the text to move.

2. Select Edit Cut, click on the Cut button on the Standard toolbar, or press Ctrl+X. The selected text is deleted from the document and placed on the Clipboard.

3. Move the insertion point to the new location.

4. Select Edit Paste, click on the Paste button on the Standard toolbar, or press Ctrl+V. The text is inserted into the new location.

Moving Text with the Mouse

You can drag selected text to a new location using the mouse. This technique is particularly convenient for small blocks of text.

1. Select the text to be moved. (Figure 8.3 gives an example.)

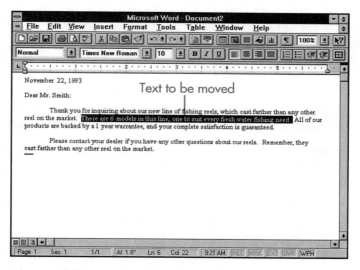

Figure 8.3 To move text, first highlight it.

2. Point at the selected text with the mouse, and press and hold the left mouse button.

3. Drag to the new location. As you drag, a dotted vertical line indicates where the text will be inserted.

4. Position the dotted line at the desired location and release the mouse button. The text is moved. Figure 8.4 shows the new position of the text that was selected in Figure 8.3.

Figure 8.4   Cut the text and paste it in the new location, or drag it to the new location with the mouse.

In this lesson, you learned how to move and copy text. In the next lesson, you'll learn how to format paragraphs.

Lesson

Formatting
Your Document

This lesson introduces you to the concept of formatting, or changing the appearance of, your document and also tells you where in the book to turn for information on specific kinds of formatting.

What Is Formatting?

The term formatting refers to changes you make in your document's appearance. Whenever you underline a word, set a paragraph off with italics, display a list as a table, or change the page margins you are working with formatting.

Formatting is an important part of many documents. An attractive and well-formatted document has a definite edge in clarity and impact over another document that has the same content but is poorly formatted. Most of the remaining lessons in this book deal with formatting; this brief lesson serves as a general introduction.

How Is Formatting Applied?

There are two methods for applying most of Word's formatting commands. The difference depends on whether you want to format text that already exists in the document, or text that you are about to type:

- To format existing text, you first select the text (as you learned in Lesson 3) and then issue the formatting command. The format change affects only the selected text.

- To format new text, move the insertion point to the location where the text is to be placed, and then issue the formatting command. The format change will affect all text that you type until you turn off or change the format command.

Where Do I Turn Next?

If it's possible, I recommend that you continue working through the book's lessons in order. If you need to find information on a particular formatting topic right away, use Table 9.1 as a guide.

Table 9.1 Formatting Topics for Further Reading

For information on	Turn to
Using fonts, underlining, boldface, and italics	Lesson 10
Changing the page margins and line spacing	Lesson 11
Using and seting tabs	Lesson 12
Modifying text alignment	Lesson 13
Adding page numbers, headers, and footers	Lesson 16
Creating numbered and bulleted lists	Lesson 18
Arranging text in columns	Lesson 19
Using Word's automatic formatting	Lesson 22

10

Formatting Characters

In this lesson, you'll learn how to apply special formatting to characters.

What Is Character Formatting?

The term character formatting refers to attributes that apply to individual characters in a document. Font, type size, underlining, italics, and boldface are examples of character formatting. A character format can apply to anything from a single letter to the entire document.

Using Fonts

What Is a Font? A font is a set of letters and characters of a particular style and size.

Plain English

The style of a font is denoted by a name, such as Times Roman or Courier. The size of a font is specified in terms of points (there are 72 points in an inch). As you enter text in a document, the Formatting toolbar displays the font name and point size currently in use. For example, in Figure 10.1, Courier 12-point is the current font.

Font name   Font size

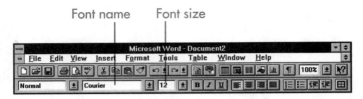

Figure 10.1   The Formatting toolbar displays the name and size of the current font.

Changing the Font of Existing Text

You can change the font style and/or size of any portion of your document, from a single character to the entire text. The exact fonts and sizes you have available will depend on your Windows installation and on the printer you are using. To change font and/or size, follow these steps:

1.   Select the text to change. If your selection currently contains only a single font and size, they are displayed on the Formatting toolbar. If it contains more than one font or size, the boxes on the toolbar will be blank.

2.   To change the font, open the font drop-down box on the Formatting toolbar. With the mouse, click on the arrow next to the box. Or, with the keyboard, press Ctrl+Shift+F and then press ↓.

3.   Select the desired font by clicking on the font name or by highlighting it and pressing Enter.

4.   To change the point size, open the point size drop-down box on the Formatting toolbar by clicking on it, and then select the desired point size. Or press Ctrl+Shift+P to access the box, and select the point size with the down arrow key.

Fast Selection!   Remember that you can quickly select an entire document by pressing Ctrl+5 (on the numeric keypad).

If you are in Page Layout view or in Normal view with Draft mode off, the screen display will immediately be updated to show the new font. In Draft mode, different fonts are not displayed on-screen, but the Formatting toolbar will display the name and size of the current font.

Fast Scrolling!   In documents with many different fonts, use Draft display mode to speed up screen scrolling.

Changing the Font of New Text

You can change the font that will be used for new text that you type by following these steps:

1. Move the insertion point to the location of the new text.

2. Follow the procedures for changing the font of existing text without first specifying a block of text.

3. Type the new text. It will appear in the newly specified font. Other text in your document will not be affected.

Bold, Underline, and Italics

The attributes boldface, italics, and/or underlining can be applied alone or in combination to any text in your document. These attributes are controlled by the toggle buttons marked **B**, *I*, and <u>U</u> on the Formatting toolbar.

Toggle Buttons These are buttons that, when selected, turn the corresponding attribute on if it was off, and off if it was on.

To apply attributes to new text that you type:

1. Move the insertion point to the location of the new text.

2. Click on the Formatting toolbar button(s) for the desired formatting, or press Ctrl+B (bold), Ctrl+I (italics), or Ctrl+U (underlining). On the Formatting toolbar, the button for each attribute that is turned on appears depressed.

3. Type the text.

4. To turn off the attribute, click on the button again or press the corresponding key combination.

To change existing text:

1. Select the text.

2. Click on the Formatting toolbar button(s) for the desired formatting, or press Ctrl+B (bold), Ctrl+I (italics), or Ctrl+U (underlining).

In Draft mode, the presence of any character formatting is indicated by underlining. In all other modes, the text appears on-screen with all formatting displayed.

In this lesson, you learned how to format characters. In the next lesson, you'll learn how to set page margins and line spacing.

Lesson

Setting Margins and Line Spacing

In this lesson, you'll learn how to set page margins and line spacing. Word provides default margins and line spacing for every template, but you can easily adjust them to suit your purposes.

Setting Left and Right Margins with the Ruler

The Ruler displayed across the top of the Word for Windows work area makes setting margins easy. You can work visually rather than thinking in terms of inches or centimeters. The Ruler is designed to be used with a mouse. To use the Ruler to change margins, you must be working in Page Layout mode (select View Page Layout).

Displaying the Ruler If your Ruler is not displayed, select View Ruler to display it.

Margins The left and right margins are the distances, respectively, between the text and the left and right edges of the page.

Margin settings affect the entire document. The white bar on the Ruler shows the current margin settings (see Figure 11.1). To change the left or right margin, point at the margin symbol on the Ruler at the left or right end of the white bar (the mouse pointer will change to a two-headed arrow). Then drag the margin symbol to the new position.

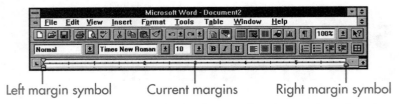

Left margin symbol   Current margins   Right margin symbol

Figure 11.1   The Ruler displays a white bar to show the current left and right margin settings.

Changing Margins   To change the margins for only a portion of a document, change the left and/or right indent (covered in Lesson 13).

Setting Left and Right Margins with a Dialog Box

If you prefer not to use the Ruler, or want to enter specific values for the margins, you can set the left and right margins using a dialog box:

1.   Select File Page Setup, and then click the Margins tab to display the **Margin** options (see Figure 11.2).

2.   In the Left box, click on the up or down arrows to increase or decrease the left margin. The numerical value is the distance between the left edge of the page and the left edge of text. The sample page in the dialog box shows what the settings will look like when printed.

3. In the Right box, click on the up or down arrows to
    increase or decrease the right margin. The value is
    the distance between the right edge of the page and
    the right edge of text.

4. Select OK.

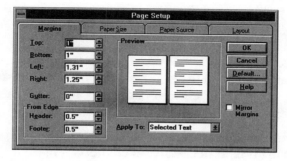

Figure 11.2 The Page Setup dialog box with the Margins
options displayed.

Setting Top and Bottom Margins

You also use the Page Setup dialog box to change the top
and bottom margins. These margins specify the distance
between text and the top and bottom of the page. As with
the left and right margins, the top and bottom margin settings affect the entire document.

1. Select File Page Setup to display the Page Setup
    dialog box.

2. If necessary, click the Margins tab to display the
    margins options.

3. In the Top box, click on the up or down arrows to
    increase or decrease the top margin. In the Bottom
    box, click on the up or down arrows to increase or
    decrease the bottom margin. The sample page in
    the dialog box shows what the settings will look
    like when printed.

4. Select OK.

Header and Footer Margins Top and bottom margins do not affect the position of headers and footers.

Changing Line Spacing

Word offers a variety of line spacing options. If you change line spacing, it affects the selected text; if there is no text selected, it affects the current paragraph and text you type at the insertion point. To change line spacing:

1. Select Format Paragraph to display the Paragraph dialog box. If necessary, click the Indents and Spacing tab (see Figure 11.3).

2. Pull down the Line Spacing list and select the desired spacing. The Single, 1.5 Lines, and Double settings are self-explanatory. The other settings are:

Exactly: Space between lines will be exactly the value, in points, that you enter in the **At** box.

At Least: Space between lines will be at least the value you enter in the **At** box; Word will increase the spacing as needed if the line contains large characters.

Multiple: Sets spacing for more than one line. In the **At** box, enter the spacing you want, making sure it accommodates the largest letters.

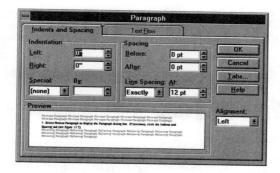

Figure 11.3 The Paragraph dialog box with the Indents and Spacing options displayed.

In this lesson, you learned how to set page margins and line spacing. The next lesson shows you how to use and set tabs.

Lesson

Setting Tabs

In this lesson, you'll learn how to use and set tabs.

What Are Tabs?

Tabs provide a way for you to control the indentation and vertical alignment of text in your document. When you press the Tab key, Word inserts a tab in the document, which moves the cursor (and any text to the right of it) to the next tab stop. By default, Word has tab stops at half-inch intervals across the width of the page. You can modify the location of tab stops, and can also control the way that text aligns at a tab stop.

Types of Tab Stops

There are four types of tab stops, each of which aligns text differently:

- Left-aligned   The left edge of text aligns at the tab stop. Word's default tab stops are all left-aligned.

- Right-aligned   The right edge of text aligns at the tab stop.

- Center-aligned   Text is centered at the tab stop.

- Decimal-aligned   The decimal point (period) is aligned at the tab stop (used for aligning columns of numbers).

Figure 12.1 illustrates the effects of the four tab alignment options. This figure also shows the four different symbols that are displayed on the Ruler to indicate the position of tab stops.

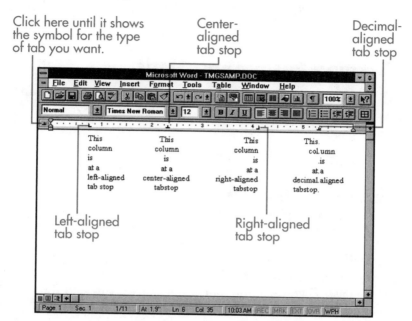

Figure 12.1   The four tab stop alignment options.

Changing the Default Tab Stops

You cannot delete the default tab stops, but you can change the spacing between them. Here are the steps to follow:

1. Select Format Tabs to display the Tabs dialog box.

2. In the Default Tab Stops box, click the up or down arrow to increase or decrease the spacing between default tab stops.

3. Select OK.

   The default tab stop spacing affects the entire document.

Getting Around It   To effectively "delete" the default tab stops, set the spacing between them to a value larger than the page width.

Creating Custom Tab Stops

If the default tab stops are not suited to your needs, you can add custom tab stops.

1. Select the paragraphs for which you want to set custom tabs. If no text is selected, the new tabs will affect text that you type at the insertion point.

2. Click the tab symbol at the left end of the Ruler until it displays the symbol for the type of tab you want to insert (refer to figure 12.1).

3. Point at the approximate tab stop location on the Ruler, and press and hold the left mouse button. A dashed vertical line will extend down through the document showing the tab stop position relative to your text.

4. Move the mouse left or right until the tab stop is at the desired location.

5. Release the mouse button.

Where's the Ruler?   If your Ruler is not displayed, select View Ruler.

When you add a custom tab stop, all of the default tab stops to the left are temporarily hidden. This ensures that the custom tab stop will take precedence.

Moving and Deleting Custom Tab Stops

Follow these steps to move a custom tab stop to a new position:

1. Point at the tab stop symbol on the Ruler.

2. Press and hold the left mouse button.

3. Drag the tab stop to the new position.

4. Release the mouse button.

To delete a custom tab stop, follow the same steps, except in step 3, drag the tab stop symbol off the Ruler.

Using Tab Leader Characters

A tab leader character is a character that is displayed in the blank space to the left of text that has been positioned using a tab. Typically, periods or hyphens are used for leader characters to create effects like that shown in Figure 12.2. This menu was created by setting a decimal-aligned tab stop at the 5.25" position with a dot leader character.

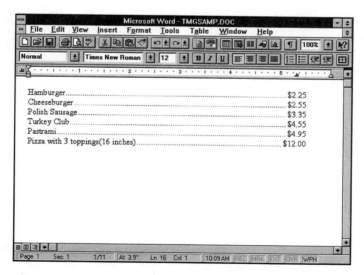

Figure 12.2   Using tabs with a leader character.

To change the leader character for a custom tab stop:

1. Point at the tab stop symbol on the Ruler and double-click. Word will display the Tabs dialog box.

2. Under Leader, select the desired leader character.

3. Select OK.

In this lesson you learned how to set and use tabs. The next lesson shows you how to align text.

Aligning Text

In this lesson, you'll learn how to use indents and justification in your documents. These features help to further customize the overall flow and appearance of your text.

Indenting Paragraphs

Word for Windows allows you to individually set the indent for the left edge, the right edge, and the first line of a paragraph.

> **What Is Indentation?** Indentation refers to the distance between the edges of a paragraph and the page margins.

Setting Indents with the Ruler

The easiest way to set indents is with the Ruler and the mouse. (If the Ruler is not displayed, select View Ruler.) The Ruler is calibrated in inches from the left margin. The Ruler elements that you use to set indents are illustrated in Figure 13.1.

To change indent positions, drag the indent symbols to the desired positions:

- To indent the first line of a paragraph, drag the First Line indent symbol.

- To indent all lines of a paragraph except the first one, drag the Other Lines indent symbol (this is called a hanging indent).

- To indent all lines of a paragraph, drag the All Lines indent symbol.

- To indent the right edge of the paragraph, drag the Right Indent symbol.

If you select one or more paragraphs first, the new indents will apply only to the selected paragraphs. If you don't select any paragraphs, the new indents will apply only to new paragraphs that you type from the insertion point forward.

Figure 13.1 The Ruler can be used to set indentation.

Quick Tab To quickly increase or decrease the left indent for the current paragraph or selected paragraphs, click the Indent button or the Outdent button on the Formatting toolbar.

Displaying the Formatting Toolbar If the Formatting toolbar is not displayed, select View Toolbars, and then select the Formatting option.

Setting Indents with a Dialog Box

If you prefer, you can set indents using a dialog box:

1. Select Format Paragraph to display the Paragraph dialog box, and then click on the Indents and Spacing tab, if necessary, to display the indents and spacing options (Figure 13.2).

2. Under Indentation, click on the up and down arrows in the Left or Right boxes to increase or decrease the indentation settings. For a first line or a hanging indent, select the indent type in the Special pull-down list, and then enter the indent amount in the By box. The sample page in the dialog box illustrates how the current settings will appear.

3. Select OK. The new settings are applied to any selected paragraphs or to new text.

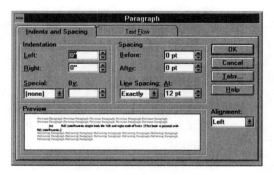

Figure 13.2   Setting Indents in the Paragraph dialog box.

Justifying Text

Word for Windows offers four justification options:

- Left justification aligns the left ends of lines.
- Right justification aligns the right ends of lines.

- Full justification aligns both the left and right ends of lines. (This book is printed with full justification.)

- Center justification centers lines between the left and right margins.

To change the justification for one or more paragraphs, first select the paragraphs to change. Then click on one of the justification buttons on the Formatting toolbar, as shown in Figure 13.3.

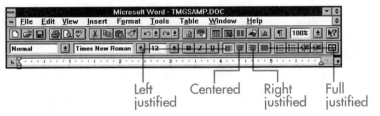

Left justified   Centered   Right justified   Full justified

Figure 13.3 Click these buttons to set text justification.

What Is Justification? Justification refers to the way in which lines on the page are aligned with the lines above and below them.

If you would rather use a dialog box to change justification, select the paragraphs and then:

1. Select Format Paragraph to display the Paragraph dialog box.

2. Open the Alignment drop-down box.

3. Select the desired alignment.

4. Select OK.

Changing Justification   If you change
justification without selecting any paragraphs, the
new justification will apply only to any new
paragraphs that you type.

In this lesson, you learned how to set indentation and
justification in your documents. In the next lesson, you'll
learn how to search for and replace text.

Lesson

Searching for and Replacing Text

In this lesson, you'll learn how to search for specific text in your document, and how to automatically replace each occurrence of it with new text.

Searching for Text

You can have Word for Windows search through your document to find occurrences of specific text. The default is to search the entire document. If there is text selected, the search will be limited to the selection.

To search for text, follow these steps:

1. Select Edit Find. The Find dialog box will be displayed, as shown in Figure 14.1.

Figure 14.1 The Find dialog box.

2. In the Find What text box, enter the text to find. This is the search template.

> **Search Template**   The *search template* is a
> model of the text you want to find.

3. (Optional) Select Find Whole Words Only to
match whole words only. With this option off, a
search template of light would match light, light-
ning, and so on. With this option on, it would
match only light.

4. (Optional) Select Match Case to require an exact
match for upper- and lowercase letters. If this
option is not selected, Word searches for text of
either case.

5. In the Search box, select All to have Word search
the entire document. You can also select Down to
have Word for Windows search from the insertion
point to the end of the document, or from the
beginning of the selected text to the end. Select Up
to search in the opposite direction.

6. Select Find Next. Word for Windows looks through
the document for text that matches the search
template. If it finds matching text, it highlights it in
the text and stops with the Find dialog box still
displayed.

7. You now can do one of two things:

- Select Find Next to continue the search for
another instance of the template.

- Press Esc to close the dialog box and return to
the document. The found text remains selected.

If, after searching only part of the document, Word
for Windows reaches the start of the document (for an
upward search) or the end of the document (for a down-
ward search), you are given the option of continuing the

search from the other end of the document. Once the entire document has been searched, a message to that effect is displayed.

Finding and Replacing Text

The Edit Replace command is used to search for instances of text, and to replace them with new text. The Edit Replace dialog box is shown in Figure 14.2.

Figure 14.2   The Replace dialog box.

Make entries in this dialog box as follows:

1. In the Find What text box, enter the target text that is to be replaced.

2. In the Replace With text box, enter the replacement text.

3. If desired, select the Find Whole Words Only, Match Case, and Search options, as explained earlier in this lesson.

4. Select Replace All to have Word for Windows go through the entire document, replacing all instances of the target text with the replacement text. You can also select Find Next to highlight the first instance of the target text.

Deleting Text   To delete the target text, leave the Replace With box blank.

If you selected Find Next, you now have three options:

- Select **Replace** to replace the highlighted text with the replacement text and then find the next instance of the target text.

- Select **Find** Next to leave the highlighted text unchanged and then find the next instance of the target text.

- Select Replace **All** to find and replace all remaining instances of the target text.

Saving Time   To save typing, use abbreviations for long words and phrases, and then later use the Replace feature to change them to final form.

Recovery!   If you make a mistake replacing text, you can recover with the Edit Undo Replace command. For this to work, you must use the Undo command immediately after the mistake (before you perform any other action).

In this lesson, you learned how to search for and optionally replace text. In the next lesson, you'll learn how to use Word for Windows templates.

Lesson

Using Templates

In this lesson, you'll learn how to use and create templates.

What Is a Template?

You may not be aware of it, but every Word for Windows document is based on a *template*. A template is a model, or pattern, that a document is based on. A template can contain boilerplate text, graphics, and formatting. It can also contain styles, glossary entries, and macros (all of which are covered in later lessons). Any document that is based upon a given template automatically contains all the elements of that template.

> **Recycle It!** Word for Windows contains some templates for your use or modification, or you can create your own from scratch. Speed up your work by creating a specialized template for document types that you use frequently.

For example, let's say you write a lot of business letters. You could create a business letter template that contains your company's name and address, logo, a salutation, and a closing. Every time you need to write a business letter, you create a new document based on the template. Such a template is shown in Figure 15.1.

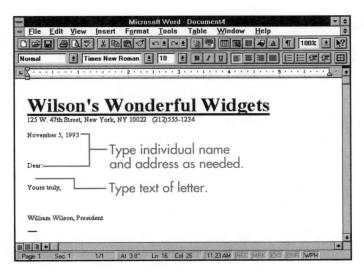

Figure 15.1 A business letter template.

By default, Word for Windows bases new documents on the NORMAL template, which is supplied with your Word for Windows package. This is a bare-bones template that contains only a few basic styles. Other Word templates are suitable for various business and personal uses. Templates are stored with a .DOT extension in the Word directory.

Using a Template

When you create a new document, you must specify the template on which you want to base it. To start a new document:

1. Select File New. The New dialog box is displayed (Figure 15.2).

2. Under **Template**, select the name of the template you want to use.

3. Select OK. The new document is created based on the selected template.

Figure 15.2 The New dialog box lists available templates.

Template Confusion? If you're not sure which template to use, select NORMAL.

Once the document is created you can modify any aspect of it, including portions that originated in the template.

Make It Quick! To quickly create a new document based on the NORMAL template, click the New Document button on the Standard toolbar.

Creating a New Template

You can create new templates to suit your specific word processing needs. To create a new template:

1. Select File New. The New dialog box is displayed.

2. Under New, select the Template option.

3. Under **Template**, be sure that NORMAL is selected.

4. Select OK. A blank document editing screen appears with a default name, such as TEMPLATE1.

5. Enter the boilerplate text and other items that you want to be part of the template.

6. Select File Save. The Save **As** dialog box is displayed.

7. In the File Name text box, enter a name of 1 to 8 characters for the template.

8. Select OK. The template is saved under the specified name, with the .DOT extension added. The new template is now available for use each time you start a new document.

Boilerplate   This is text that appears the same in all documents of a certain type.

Modifying an Existing Template

You can retrieve any existing template from disk and modify it. You can then save it under the original name or a new name. To modify a template:

1. Select File Open. The Open dialog box is displayed.

2. Open the List Files of **Type** drop-down box and select Document Templates.

3. If necessary, select a different drive and directory in the **Drives** and **Directories** lists (templates are usually stored in the C:\WINWORD6\TEMPLATE directory).

4. Under File Name, select the template that you want to modify.

5. Make the desired modifications and additions to the template.

6. To save the modified template under its original name, select File Save. To save the modified template under a new name, select File Save As and enter a new template name.

If you modify the text in a template, those changes will not be reflected in documents that were based on the template as it was before the changes were made.

In this lesson, you learned about Word for Windows templates. In the next lesson, you'll learn how to create and use page numbers, headers, and footers.

Lesson

Page Numbers, Headers, and Footers

In this lesson, you'll learn how to add page numbers, headers, and footers to your documents.

Adding Page Numbers

Many documents, particularly long ones, benefit from having numbered pages. Word for Windows offers complete flexibility in the placement and format of page numbers. To add page numbers to your document:

1. Select Insert Page Numbers. The Page Numbers dialog box is displayed, as shown in Figure 16.1.

2. Pull down the Position list and select the desired position on the page: Top of Page (Header) or Bottom of Page (Footer).

3. Pull down the Alignment list and select Left, Center, or Right. You can also select Inside or Outside if you're printing two-sided pages and want the page numbers positioned near (Inside) or away from (Outside) the binding.

4. The default number format is Arabic numerals (1, 2, 3, and so on). To select a different format (for example, i, ii, iii), select Format and select the desired format.

5. Select OK.

Figure 16.1   The Page Numbers dialog box.

When you add a page number using the above procedure, Word for Windows makes your selection part of the
document's header or footer. Headers and footers are explained next.

What Are Headers and Footers?

A header or footer is text that is printed at the top (a header)
or bottom (a footer) of every page of a document. A header
or footer can be as simple as the page number, or it can
contain chapter titles, authors' names, or any other information you desire. Word for Windows offers several header/
footer options:

- The same header/footer on every page of the
  document.

- One header/footer on the first page of the document
  and a different header/footer on all other pages.

- One header/footer on odd-numbered pages and a
  different header/footer on even-numbered pages.

> **Headers and Footers**   The header is at the
> top of the page, and the footer is at the bottom.

Adding or Editing a Header or Footer

To add a header or footer to your document, or to edit an
existing header or footer, follow these steps:

1. Select View Header and Footer. Word displays the current page's header, enclosed by a nonprinting dashed line (Figure 16.2). Regular document text is dimmed, and the Header and Footer toolbar is displayed. On the toolbar, click the Switch button to switch between the header and footer.

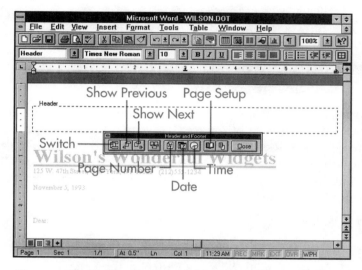

Figure 16.2 The Header and Footer toolbar is displayed when you select View Header and Footer.

2. Enter the header or footer text and formatting using the regular Word editing techniques.

3. If you want the date, time, or page number inserted, click the appropriate button on the toolbar.

4. Click the Show Next and Show Previous buttons on the Header and Footer toolbar to switch between the various sections. As you edit, each header or footer will be labeled (for example, "First Page Header," "Odd Page Footer," and so on).

5.   When you are finished, click the Close button on the toolbar to return to the document.

> **Deleting a Header or Footer**   To delete a header or footer, follow the steps above for editing the header or footer. Select all of the text in the header or footer, and press Del.

Creating Different Headers and Footers for Different Pages

Normally, Word displays the same header and footer on all pages of a document. However, you can tell Word to print one header or footer on the first page and a different one on all other pages. Or you can print one header or footer on all odd-numbered pages and another on all even-numbered pages. To activate one or both of these options:

1.   Select View Header and Footer.

2.   Click the Page Setup button on the Header and Footer toolbar. Word will display the Page Setup dialog box. Click the Layout tab, if necessary, to display the page layout options (Figure 16.3).

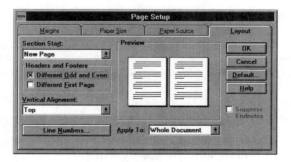

Figure 16.3   The Page Setup dialog box.

3. In the Headers and Footers section of the dialog box, turn on the Different Odd and Even option and/or the Different First Page option.

4. Select OK to close the Page Setup dialog box.

In this lesson, you learned how to add page numbers, headers, and footers to a document. The next lesson shows you how to proof and improve your document using the Speller and Thesaurus features.

Lesson

Proofing Your Document

In this lesson, you'll learn to use Word for Windows Speller and Thesaurus utilities to help proof your document.

Using the Spelling Checker

The spelling checker lets you verify and correct the spelling of words in your document. Word for Windows checks words against a standard dictionary and lets you know when it encounters an unknown word. You then can ignore it, change it, or add it to the dictionary.

To check spelling in a portion of a document, select the text to check. To check the entire document, first move the insertion point to the start of the document by pressing Ctrl+Home. Then:

1. Select Tools Spelling, press F7, or click on the Spelling check button on the Standard toolbar.

2. If a word is found in the document that is not in the dictionary, it is highlighted in the text and the Spelling dialog box is displayed (see Figure 17.1).

3. In the Spelling dialog box, the Not in Dictionary box displays the word that was not found in the dictionary. If the spelling checker has found any likely replacements, they are listed in the Suggestions list box. In the dialog box, you have the following options:

- To ignore the highlighted word and continue, select Ignore.

- To ignore the highlighted word and any other instances of it in the document, select Ignore All.

- To change the highlighted word, type the new spelling in the Change To box or highlight the desired replacement word in the Suggestions list box. Then select Change (to change the current instance of the word) or Change All (to change all instances of this word in the document).

- To add the word to the dictionary, select Add.

4. The spelling checker proceeds to check the rest of the document. When it is finished checking, it displays a message to that effect. To cancel spell checking at any time, select Cancel in the Spelling dialog box.

Figure 17.1 The Spelling dialog box.

Fast Check! To check the spelling of a single word, double-click on the word to select it, and then press F7.

The Thesaurus

A thesaurus provides you with synonyms and antonyms for words in your document. Using the Thesaurus can help you avoid repetition in your writing (and can also improve your vocabulary). To use the Thesaurus:

1. Place the insertion point on the word of interest in your document.

2. Select Tools Thesaurus or press Shift+F7.

3. The Thesaurus dialog box opens (Figure 17.2). This dialog box has several components.

   - Looked Up displays the word of interest.

   - The Meanings box lists alternative meanings for the word. If the word was not found, Word displays an Alphabetical List box instead; this list contains a list of words with spellings similar to the selected word.

   - If the Thesaurus found one or more meanings for the word, the dialog box displays the Replace with Synonym list showing synonyms for the currently highlighted meaning of the word. If meanings were not found, the dialog box displays a Replace with Related Word list.

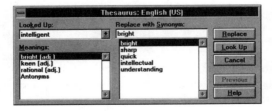

Figure 17.2 The Thesaurus dialog box.

4. While the Thesaurus dialog box is displayed, there are several actions you can take:

- To find synonyms for the highlighted word in the Replace with Synonym list or the Replace with Related Words list (depending on which one is displayed), select Look Up.

- To find synonyms for a word in the Meanings list, select the word and then select Look Up.

- For some words, the Thesaurus will display the term Antonyms in the Meanings list. To display antonyms for the selected word, highlight the term Antonyms and then select Look Up.

5. To replace the word in the document with the word that is highlighted in the Replace with Synonym list or the Replace with Related Word list, select Replace.

6. To close the thesaurus without making any changes to the document, select Cancel.

Prevent Repetition Use the Thesaurus to avoid repeating words in your document.

In this lesson you learned how to use the Speller and Thesaurus to proof your document. The next lesson shows you how to create numbered and bulleted lists.

Lesson 18

Creating Numbered and Bulleted Lists

In this lesson you'll learn how to create numbered and bulleted lists in your document.

Why Use Numbered and Bulleted Lists?

Numbered and bulleted lists are useful formatting tools for setting off lists of information in a document; you've seen plenty of both in this book! Word for Windows can create these elements automatically. Use bulleted lists for items of information that are related, but are not in any particular order. Use numbered lists for items that are in a specific order. Figure 18.1 shows examples of numbered and bulleted lists.

When you create a list, each paragraph is considered a separate list item and receives its own number or bullet.

Creating a Numbered or Bulleted List

To create a numbered or bulleted list from existing text, follow these steps:

1. Select the paragraphs that you want in the list.

2. Select Format Bullets and Numbering to display the Bullets and Numbering dialog box.

3. Depending on the type of list you want, click on the Bulleted tab or the Numbered tab. Figure 18.2 shows the Numbered style options, and Figure 18.3 shows the Bulleted style options.

4. Click the bulleting or numbering option that you want.

5. Select OK.

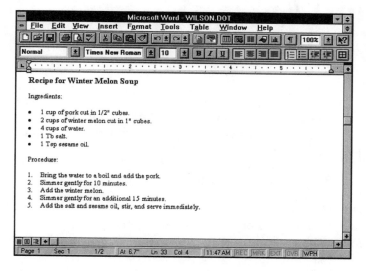

Figure 18.1 Word can automatically create numbered and bulleted lists like these.

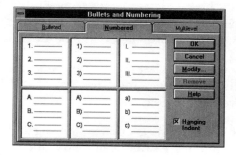

Figure 18.2 List numbering style options displayed in the Bullets and Numbering dialog box.

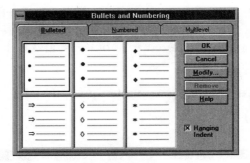

Figure 18.3 List bulleting style options displayed in the Bullets and Numbering dialog box.

To create a numbered or bulleted list as you type:

1. Move the insertion point to the location for the list. Press Enter, if necessary, to start a new paragraph.

2. Select Format Bullets and Numbering to display the Bullets and Numbering dialog box.

3. Depending on the type of list you want, click on the Bulleted tab or the Numbered tab.

4. Click the bulleting or numbering style that you want.

5. Select OK.

6. Type in the list elements, pressing Enter at the end of each paragraph. Each paragraph will be automatically numbered or bulleted as it is added.

7. At the end of the last paragraph, press Enter. Word will insert an extra, empty list item that will be removed in the next step.

8. Select Format Bullets and Numbering to display the Bullets and Numbering dialog box, and then select Remove.

There's a Quicker Way You can create a numbered or bulleted list quickly, in the default style, by highlighting the paragraphs and clicking the Numbered List or Bulleted List button on the Standard toolbar.

Undoing a Numbered or Bulleted List

Follow these steps to remove bullets or numbers from a list:

1. Select the paragraphs from which you want to remove bullets or numbering. This can be the entire list or just part of it.

2. Select Format Bullets and Numbering to display the Bullets and Numbering dialog box.

3. Select Remove.

Adding Items to Numbered and Bulleted Lists

You can add new items to a numbered or bulleted list by following these steps:

1. Move the insertion point to the location in the list where you want the new item.

2. Press Enter to start a new paragraph. Word automatically inserts a new bullet or number and renumbers the list items as needed.

3. Enter the new text.

4. Repeat as many times as needed.

This lesson showed you how to use numbered and bulleted lists. In the next lesson you'll learn how to arrange text in columns.

Lesson

Arranging Text in Columns

In this lesson you'll learn how to use columns in your documents.

Why Use Columns?

Columns are commonly used in newsletters, brochures, and similar documents. The shorter lines of text provided by columns are easier to read, and also provide greater flexibility in formatting a document with graphics, tables, and so on. Word for Windows makes it easy to use columns in your documents. Figure 19.1 shows a document formatted with three columns.

Figure 19.1 A document formatted with three columns.

Note that the Word for Windows columns feature creates *newspaper* style columns, in which the text flows to the bottom of one column and then continues at the top of the next column on the page. For side-by-side paragraphs, such as you would need in a resume or a script, use Word's Table feature, covered in Lesson 23.

Creating Columns

Word for Windows has four predefined column layouts:

- Two equal width columns

- Three equal width columns

- Two unequal width columns with the wider column on the left

- Two unequal width columns with the wider column on the right

You can apply any of these column formats to all or part of a document, to selected text, or from the insertion point onward. Here are the steps to follow:

1. If you want only a part of the document in columns, select the text that you want in columns, or move the insertion point to the location where you want columns to begin.

2. Select Format Columns to display the Columns dialog box (Figure 19.2).

3. Under Presets, click the column format that you want.

4. Pull down the Apply To list and specify the extent to which the columns should apply.

5. Turn on the Line Between option to display a vertical line between columns.

6. Select OK.

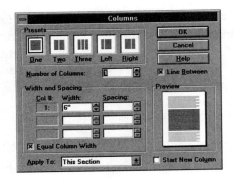

Figure 19.2   The Columns dialog box.

Toolbar Shortcut   To display selected text or the entire document in one to four equal width columns, click the Columns button on the Standard toolbar, and then drag over the desired number of columns.

Screen Display of Columns

To view columns on-screen while you are editing, you must be working in Page Layout mode. In Normal mode, Word displays only a single column at a time. To switch to Page Layout mode, select View Page Layout.

Modifying Columns

Here are the steps to follow to modify existing columns:

1.   Highlight the text in columns that you want to modify.

2.   Select Format Columns to display the Columns dialog box. The options in the dialog box will reflect the current settings for the selected columns.

3. Make changes to the column settings as desired.

4. Select OK.

Turning Columns Off

To convert multiple-column text back to normal one-column text, follow these steps:

1. Select the text that you want to change from multiple columns to a single column.

2. Select Format Columns to display the Columns dialog box.

3. Under Presets, select the One style option.

4. Select OK.

This lesson showed you how to arrange text in columns. The next lesson shows you how to use styles.

Lesson

Using Styles

In this lesson, you'll learn how to use styles in your documents.

Understanding Styles

A style is a collection of formatting specifications that has been assigned a name and saved. You can quickly apply a style to any text in any Word for Windows document. Applying a style is a lot faster than manually applying each individual formatting element, and has the added advantage of assuring consistency. If you later modify a style's formatting, all paragraphs in the document to which that style has been assigned will automatically change to reflect the new definition.

What Is a Style? A *style* is a named grouping of paragraph and character formatting that can be reused.

Word has two types of styles:

- *Paragraph* styles apply to entire paragraphs, and can include all aspects of formatting that affect a paragraph's appearance: font, line spacing, indents, tab stops, borders, and so on.

- *Character* styles apply to any text, and can include any formatting that applies to individual characters: font name and size, underlining, boldface, etc. (in other words, any of the formats that are assigned via the Font command on the Format menu).

The formatting of character styles is applied in addition to whatever formatting the text already has. For example, if you apply a character style defined as boldface to a word in a sentence that is already formatted as italics, the word will be displayed in bold italics.

Word for Windows comes with several predefined paragraph and character styles. You can use these styles as-is, or you can modify them to suit your needs and create your own new styles. These topics are covered in this lesson and the next one.

Viewing Style Names

The Style box at the left end of the Formatting toolbar displays the current style name. If there is text selected or if the insertion point is in text that has a character style applied, the Style box displays the character style name. Otherwise, it displays the paragraph style of the current paragraph.

Default Style   Every paragraph in a Word document has a paragraph style applied to it; the default is Word's predefined Normal style.

Word for Windows can also display the name of the paragraph style assigned to each paragraph in your document. This is shown in Figure 20.1. Style names can be displayed only in Normal or Outline view.

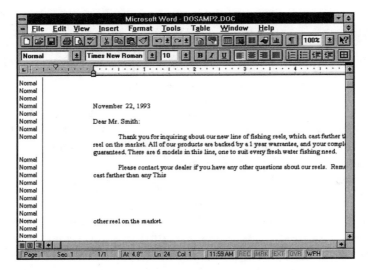

Figure 20.1 A screen with paragraph style names displayed.

To display the style name area:

1. Select Tools Options. Then, if necessary, click the View tab to display the view options.

2. In the Window section, find the Style Area Width box. Click on the up arrow to set a positive width for the style name area. A setting of 0.5" is good for most situations. To hide the style name area, enter a width of 0.

3. Select OK. The screen now displays paragraph style names to the left of the text.

Use Your Mouse   While the Style Name Area is displayed, you can point at its right border with the mouse and drag it to a new width.

Assigning a Style

To assign a style to text:

1. To assign a paragraph style to multiple paragraphs, select the paragraphs. For a single paragraph, place the insertion point anywhere inside the paragraph. To assign a character style, select the text.

2. Open the Style drop-down box on the Formatting toolbar. With the mouse, click on the arrow next to the box. With the keyboard, press Ctrl+Shift+S and then press the down arrow.

3. The box lists all available styles. Select the desired style. With the mouse, click on the style name. With the keyboard, use the arrow keys to highlight the style name, and then press Enter.

4. The style is applied to the specified text.

Looking at the Style Box   In the Style box, paragraph styles are listed in boldface, and character styles are listed in normal text.

Deleting Styles   To remove a character style from text, select the text and apply the character style "Default Paragraph Font."

In this lesson, you learned how to use paragraph and character styles to format your document. The next lesson shows you how to create your own styles.

Lesson 21

Creating Your Own Styles

In this lesson, you'll learn how to create your own styles and how to modify existing styles.

Creating a New Style

In the previous lesson, you learned how useful styles can be for formatting your documents. You also learned the difference between paragraph styles (which apply to entire paragraphs) and character styles (which apply to any section of text). You can use Word's predefined styles, or you can create your own.

Follow these steps to create a new paragraph style:

1. Find a paragraph to which you want the new style applied.

2. Format the paragraph in the new style that you want to apply to other paragraphs later on.

3. With the insertion point anywhere in the paragraph, click on the Style box.

4. Enter the new style name and press Enter.

In step 4, be sure not to enter the name of an existing style. If you do, that style's formatting will be applied to the paragraph and the formatting changes that you made will be lost. (If you do this accidentally, you can recover the formatting by issuing the **Edit Undo** command immediately.)

Here's how to create a new character style:

1. Select Format Style to display the Style dialog box.

2. In the dialog box, select New. The New Style dialog box is displayed (Figure 21.1).

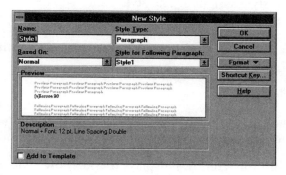

Figure 21.1   The New Style dialog box.

3. Pull down the Style Type list and select Character.

4. Select the Name box and type in the name for the new style.

5. Click on the Format button and select Font. Word displays the Font dialog box.

6. Specify the formatting that you want the new style to have, and then select OK to return to the New Style dialog box.

7. Select OK, and then select Close.

Modifying a Style

You can change the formatting associated with any paragraph style. When you do so, all text in the document that has the style assigned will be modified. Follow these steps to modify an existing style:

1. To modify a paragraph style, select a paragraph formatted with the style. To modify a character style, select text (at least one character) that has that style assigned. The style name will be displayed in the Style box on the Formatting toolbar.

2. Make the desired changes to the text's formatting.

3. Be sure that the original text or paragraph is still selected.

4. Click on the Style box on the Formatting toolbar, and then click anywhere in the document window.

5. Word for Windows displays the Reapply Style dialog box. Select the option Redefine the style using the selection as an example? if it is not already selected.

6. Select OK. The style is redefined with the new formatting.

You can also modify an existing style using dialog boxes. To do so, follow these steps:

1. Select Format Style to display the Style dialog box, shown in Figure 21.2.

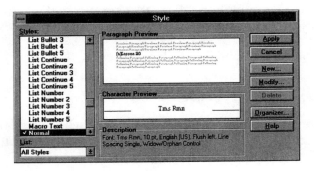

Figure 21.2 The Style dialog box.

2.   In the Styles list, highlight the name of the style you want to modify.

3.   Select Modify to display the Modify Style dialog box.

4.   Select Format. From the list that is displayed, select the type of formatting you want to modify. The number of formatting types available on the list depends on whether you are modifying a Paragraph style or a Character style.

5.   Word will display the appropriate formatting dialog box. Make the desired changes, and then select OK. You will return to the Modify Style dialog box.

6.   Repeat steps 4 and 5 as many times as necessary to make all the desired modifications to the style's formatting.

7.   From the Modify Styles dialog box, select OK. You return to the Style dialog box.

8.   Select Close.

In this lesson, you learned how to create and modify styles. The next lesson shows you how to use automatic formatting.

Lesson 22

Using Automatic Formatting

In this lesson, you'll learn how to have Word format your document automatically.

What Is Automatic Formatting?

Automatic formatting refers to Word's ability to analyze the structure of a document and recognize certain common elements, such as body text, headings, bulleted lists, and quotations. Word will then apply appropriate styles to the various text elements to create an attractively formatted document (for information on styles, refer to Lessons 20 and 21). You can accept or reject all or part of the automatically applied format, and can later make any desired modifications to the document. In addition to applying styles, automatic formatting can remove extra "returns" between paragraphs, create bulleted lists, and more.

Applying Automatic Formatting

You can apply automatic formatting to all or part of a document:

1. To format part of a document, select the text. Otherwise, position the insertion point anywhere in the document.

2. Select Format AutoFormat and select OK. Word analyzes and reformats the document, and displays the AutoFormat dialog box shown in Figure 22.1.

Figure 22.1   Use the AutoFormat dialog box to accept or reject the formatting applied by the AutoFormat command.

3. Use the vertical scroll bar to scroll through the document and examine the new formatting. The dialog box will remain displayed; grab its title bar and drag it to another location if it is blocking your view of the document.

4. Select Reject All to undo all formatting changes and return the document to its original state. Select Accept to accept all the changes. Select Review Changes if you want to review the changes and accept or reject them individually (described in detail in the following section).

Reviewing the Formatting Changes

If you select Review Changes from the AutoFormat dialog box, you can scroll through the document, examine each individual formatting change, and then either accept it or reject it. The Review AutoFormat Changes dialog box will be displayed during this procedure, as shown in Figure 22.2. Scroll through the document using the vertical scroll bar. Word indicates the changes that were made using the marks shown in Table 22.1.

Table 22.1 Word Indicates Formatting Changes Made

Change made	Mark displayed
New style applied to the paragraph	Blue paragraph mark
Paragraph mark deleted	Red paragraph mark
Text or spaces deleted	Strikethru
Characters added	Underline
Text or formatting changed	Vertical bar in left margin

Figure 22.2 Accept or reject individual formatting changes in the Review AutoFormat Changes dialog box.

As you examine the document, make selections in the Review AutoFormat Changes dialog box as follows:

- Select Find → or ← Find to highlight the next or previous change.

- Select Reject to undo the highlighted change.

- Select Undo Last to reverse the last Reject command (restoring the rejected change).

- Select Hide Marks to display the document as it would appear if all remaining changes were accepted. Select Show Marks to return to revisions display.

- Turn on the Find Next after Reject option to have Word automatically find the next revision after you reject the current one.

*   Select **Cancel** to accept the remaining revisions and return to the AutoFormat dialog box.

Setting the AutoFormat Options

The AutoFormat feature has a number of settings that control which document elements it will modify. You can change these options to suit your preferences:

1.   Select Tools Options to display the Options dialog box.

2.   Click the AutoFormat tab to display the AutoFormat options (Figure 22.3).

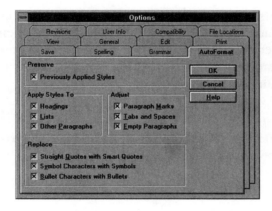

Figure 22.3   Use the Options dialog box screen to set Word's AutoFormat options.

3.   Turn options on or off to control which document elements the AutoFormat command will affect.

4.   Select OK.

This lesson showed you how to use Word's automatic formatting capability. In the next lesson, you'll learn how to use tables.

Lesson

Tables

In this lesson, you'll learn how to add tables to your documents.

Uses for Tables

A *table* lets you organize information in a row and column format. Each entry in a table, called a *cell*, is independent of all other entries. You control the number of rows and columns in a table and the formatting of each cell. A table cell can contain anything except another table.

> **Why Tables?** Use tables for columns of numbers, lists, and anything else that requires a row and column arrangement.

Inserting a Table

You can insert a new, empty table at any location within your document. Just follow these steps:

1. Move the insertion point to where you want the table.

2. Select Table Insert Table. The Insert Table dialog box is displayed, as shown in Figure 23.1.

Figure 23.1   The Insert Table dialog box.

3.   In the Number of Columns and Number of Rows boxes, click the arrows or enter the number of rows and columns the table should have. (You can adjust these numbers later if you need to.)

4.   In the Column Width box, select the column width. Select Auto to have the page width evenly divided among the specified number of columns.

5.   Select OK. A blank table is created with the insertion point in the first cell. Figure 23.2, for example, shows a blank table with 4 rows and 3 columns.

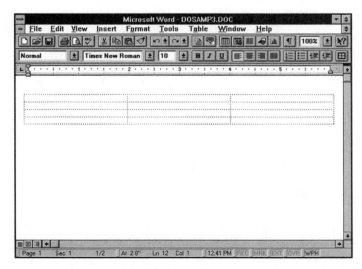

Figure 23.2   A blank table with 4 rows and 3 columns.

Using the Toolbar   To quickly insert a table, click the Table button on the Standard toolbar, and then drag over the desired number of rows and columns.

Working in a Table

When the insertion point is in a table cell, you can enter and edit text as you would in the rest of the document. Text entered in a cell automatically wraps to the next line within the column width. Navigate through a table using the special key combinations described in Table 23.1.

Table 23.1   Moving Through a Table

Press	To move
Tab	To the next cell in a row.
Shift+Tab	To the previous cell in a row.
Alt+Home	To the first cell in the current row.
Alt+PgUp	To the top cell in the current column.
Alt+End	To the last cell in the current row.
Alt+PgDn	To the last cell in the current column.

If the insertion point is at the edge of a cell, you can also use the arrow keys to move between cells.

Formatting a Table

Once you've created a table and entered some information, you can format it to suit your needs.

Deleting and Inserting Cells, Rows, and Columns

You can delete individual cells, erasing their contents and leaving a blank cell. You can also delete entire rows and columns. When you do so, columns to the right or rows below move to fill in for the deleted row or column.

> **Fast Select!**   To select an entire cell, click in the left margin of the cell, between the text and the cell border. The mouse pointer changes to an arrow when it's in this area.

To delete the contents of a cell:

1. Select the cell.

2. Press Del.

To delete an entire row or column:

1. Move the insertion point to any cell in the row or column to be deleted.

2. Select Table Delete Cells. A dialog box is displayed.

3. In the dialog box, select Delete Entire Row or Delete Entire Column.

4. Select OK. The row or column is deleted.

To insert a row or column:

1. Move the insertion point to a cell to the right or below the location of the new column or row.

2. Select Table Select Row to insert a row or Table Select Column to insert a column. The entire row or column becomes selected.

3. Select Table Insert Columns to insert a new, blank column to the left of the selected column. Select Table Insert Rows to insert a new, blank row above the selected row.

The Commands Vary!   The commands on the Table menu change according to circumstances. For example, if you have selected a column in a table, the Insert Columns command is displayed but the Insert Rows command is not.

To insert a new row at the bottom of the table:

1. Move the insertion point to the last cell in the last row of the table.

2. Press Tab. A new row is added at the bottom of the table.

Changing Column Width

You can quickly change the width of a column with the mouse:

1. Point at the right border of the column you want to change. The mouse pointer changes to thin vertical lines with arrowheads pointing left and right.

2. Drag the column border to the desired width.

You can also use a dialog box to change column widths:

1. Move the insertion point to any cell in the column you want to change.

2. Select Table Cell Height and Width. The Cell Height and Width dialog box is displayed.

3. In the dialog box, click the Column tab if necessary to display the column options.

4. In the Width of Column box, enter the desired column width, or click on the up and down arrows to change the setting.

5. Change the value in the Space Between Columns box to modify spacing between columns.

6. Select Next Column or Previous Column to change the settings for other columns in the table.

7. Select OK. The table changes to reflect the new column settings.

Automatic Table Formatting

The AutoFormat command makes it a snap to apply attractive formatting to any table:

1. Place the insertion point anywhere in the table.

2. Select Table Table AutoFormat. The Table Auto-Format dialog box is displayed (see Figure 23.3).

3. The Formats box lists the available table formats. As you scroll through the list, the Preview box shows the appearance of the highlighted format.

4. In the lower section of the dialog box are a number of formatting options. Select and deselect options as necessary until the preview shows the table appearance you want.

5. Select OK. The selected formatting is applied to the table.

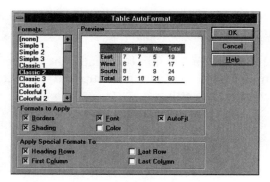

Figure 23.3   Use the Table AutoFormat dialog box to apply table formatting.

In this lesson, you learned how to add tables to your documents. In the next lesson, you'll learn how to add graphics to your document.

Lesson 24

Adding Graphics to Your Documents

In this lesson, you'll learn how to add graphics to your documents.

Adding a Graphics Image

A graphics image is a picture that is stored on disk in a graphics file. Word for Windows can utilize graphics files created by a wide variety of applications, including Lotus 1-2-3, Windows Metafiles, Micrografx Designer, and AutoCAD. In addition, your Word installation includes a small library of clip art images that you can use in your documents. Figure 24.1 shows a document with a graphic image.

To add a graphics image to a Word for Windows document, follow these steps:

1. Move the insertion point to the location for the graphic.

2. Select Insert Picture. The Insert Picture dialog box is displayed, as shown in Figure 24.2.

3. If necessary, use the Directories and Drives boxes to specify the drive and directory where the graphics file is located.

4.   The File Name box normally lists all graphics files in the specified directory. To have the list restricted to certain types of graphics files, open the List Files of Type drop-down box and select the desired file type.

5.   In the File Name box, type the name of the file to insert, or select the file name from the list.

6.   To preview the picture in the Preview box, select the Preview Picture option.

7.   Select the Link to File option if you want the graphic in your document updated if the graphics file on disk changes.

8.   Select OK. The graphic is inserted into your document.

Figure 24.1   A document with a displayed graphic.

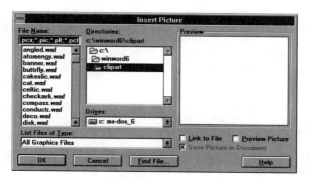

Figure 24.2 The Insert Picture dialog box.

Displaying Graphics

The display of graphics images can slow down screen scrolling. If you're working on the document text and don't need to see the images, you can speed up screen display by displaying empty rectangles called *placeholders* in place of the images. In addition, if you selected the Link to File option when inserting the graphic file, Word for Windows inserts a field code in the document. The screen will display this code instead of the picture when field codes are displayed. Here's how to control the display of graphics:

1. Select Tools Options to display the Options dialog box.

2. If necessary, click the View tab to display the View options.

3. In the Show section, turn the Picture Placeholders and Field Codes options on or off as desired.

4. Select OK.

The screen display of placeholders or field codes does not affect printing, which will always include the actual graphics.

Fast Takes   When working on a document that contains graphics, you can speed up screen display and scrolling by displaying placeholders for the graphics.

Selecting a Graphic

Before you can work with a graphic in your document, you must select it:

- With the mouse, click on the graphic.

- With the keyboard, position the insertion point immediately to the left of the graphic, and then press Shift+→.

When a graphic is selected, it is surrounded by eight small black squares called *sizing handles*.

Cropping and Resizing a Graphic

You can resize a graphic in your document, displaying the entire picture at a different size. You can also crop a graphic, hiding portions of the picture that you don't want to show. To resize or crop a graphic:

1. Select the graphic.

2. Point at one of the resizing handles. The mouse pointer will change to a double-headed arrow.

3. To resize, press the left mouse button and drag the handle until the outline of the graphic is at the desired size. You can either enlarge or shrink the graphic.

4. To crop, press and hold Shift. Then press the left mouse button and drag a handle toward the center of the graphic.

Deleting, Moving, and Copying Graphics

To delete a graphic, select it and press Del. To move or copy a graphic:

1. Select the graphic.

2. Press Ctrl+C or select Edit Copy (to copy the graphic), or press Ctrl+X or select Edit Cut (to move the graphic). Alternatively, you can click on the Copy or Cut button on the Standard toolbar.

3. Move the insertion point to the new location for the graphic.

4. Press Ctrl+V, select Edit Paste, or click on the Paste button on the Standard toolbar.

In this lesson, you learned how to add graphics to your documents. The next lesson shows you how to use AutoText entries.

Lesson 25

Using AutoText Entries

In this lesson, you'll learn how to use the AutoText feature.

What Is AutoText?

The AutoText feature lets you define and save a collection of commonly used words, phrases, or sentences to be inserted into a document so you don't have to type them each time. You insert an AutoText entry in the document by typing a short abbreviation or name that you assigned to it. Typical uses for AutoText entries are your company name, the closing sentence for a business letter, and your name and title. An AutoText entry can contain just text or text along with special formatting.

Creating an AutoText Entry

To create an AutoText entry, you must first type it into your document and add any special formatting that you want included. Then follow these steps:

1. Select the text for the AutoText entry. If you want its formatting included as well, be sure to include the ending paragraph mark in the selection.

2. Select Edit AutoText. The AutoText dialog box is displayed (see Figure 25.1).

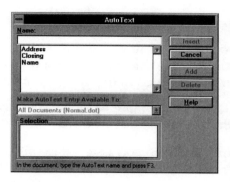

Figure 25.1   The AutoText dialog box.

3. In the Name text box, enter a name or abbreviation for the AutoText entry, or accept the name suggested by Word. This should be a short name that is descriptive of the entry. You will later use this name when inserting the AutoText entry into documents.

4. If your document is based on any template besides NORMAL, you have two choices as to where the AutoText entry should be stored. Pull down the Make AutoText Entry Available To list, and then choose one of these options:

- Select All Documents to have the AutoText entry available for all future documents.

- Select Documents Based On to have the entry available only for future documents created with the current template.

5. Select Add.

Return Address   Save time by creating an AutoText entry that contains your name and address.

Inserting an AutoText Entry

You have two options for inserting an AutoText entry into your document. The first method is fastest if you remember the name that you assigned to the AutoText entry.

1. Move the insertion point to the location where you want the AutoText entry inserted.

2. Type the name that you assigned to the AutoText entry, but do not press Enter. Be sure the AutoText name is preceded by a space if it is not the first item on a line.

3. Press F3. The corresponding AutoText entry is inserted in place of its name.

> **Quick Access**   To insert an AutoText entry, type the entry name and press F3.

If you are not sure of the AutoText entry name, follow this procedure:

1. Move the insertion point to the location where you want the AutoText entry inserted.

2. Select Edit AutoText. The AutoText dialog box is displayed, with a list of defined AutoText entries.

3. Type the name of the desired AutoText entry, or select it from the list.

4. Select the Formatted Text option to insert the AutoText entry with its formatting. Select the Plain Text option to insert the AutoText text without formatting.

5. Select Insert.

Modifying an AutoText Entry

You can modify an existing AutoText entry. Such modifications will not affect previous instances of the AutoText entry in your documents.

1. Insert the AutoText entry into a document as described earlier in this lesson.

2. Edit the text and/or formatting as desired.

3. Select the newly edited text, including the paragraph mark if you want the formatting included in the AutoText entry.

4. Select Edit AutoText. From the list of entries, select the name of the AutoText entry that you are modifying.

5. Select Add.

6. When asked whether to redefine the AutoText entry, select Yes.

Deleting an AutoText Entry

You can delete an unneeded AutoText entry from the AutoText list. Deleting an AutoText entry has no effect on instances of the entry that were inserted previously.

1. Select Edit AutoText.

2. Type the AutoText entry name or select it from the list.

3. Select Delete. The entry is deleted.

In this lesson you learned how to use AutoText entries. The next lesson shows you how to open more than one document at the same time.

Lesson

Opening Multiple Documents

In this lesson, you'll learn how to open multiple documents in Word for Windows.

Why Use Multiple Documents?

You may feel that working on one document at a time is quite enough. In some situations, however, the ability to work on multiple documents at the same time can be very useful. You can refer to one document while working on another, and you can copy and move text from one document to another. Word for Windows can have as many as nine documents open simultaneously.

Starting a New Document

You can start a new document while you're working on an existing document. To do so, follow these procedures:

1. With the original document displayed on-screen, select File New. The New dialog box is displayed (see Figure 26.1).

2. Select the Document option if it is not already selected.

3. In the Template list, select the template on which you want to base the new document.

4. Select OK. A new, blank document window is opened over the existing document. The new document is assigned a default name by Word for Windows, such as DOCUMENT1, DOCUMENT2, and so on.

5. Enter text and edit the new document in the normal fashion. The original document remains in memory. If you close the new document, you will be returned to the original document.

Figure 26.1   The New dialog box.

Fast Open!   To open a new document based on the NORMAL template, click on the File New button on the Standard toolbar.

Opening an Existing Document

While working in one document, you can also open another existing document. Simply select File Open or click on the File Open button on the Standard toolbar, and then select the name of the document you want to open and select OK. A new window opens, displaying the document. Both the newly opened document and the original document are in memory, and can be edited, printed, and so on.

Switching Between Documents

When you have multiple documents open at one time, only
one of them can be active at a given moment. The active
document is displayed on-screen and is the only one affected
by editing commands. You can have as many as nine documents open at the same time, and you can switch between
them at will.

To switch between open documents:

1. Select Window. The Window menu lists all open
    documents, with a check mark next to the name of
    the currently active document.

2. Select the name of the document you want to make
    active. You can either click on the document name
    with the mouse or press the key corresponding to
    the number listed next to the name on the menu.

3. The selected document becomes active and is
    displayed on-screen.

Next Please!   To cycle to the next open
document, press Ctrl+F6.

In this lesson, you learned how to open multiple documents. The next lesson shows you how to work with multiple documents.

Lesson

Working with Multiple Documents

In this lesson, you'll learn how to work with multiple documents in Word for Windows.

Moving and Copying Text Between Documents

When you have more than one document open, you can move and copy text between documents. Follow these steps:

1. Make the source document active and select the text that is to be moved or copied.

2. Press Ctrl+X or select Edit Cut (to move the text), or press Ctrl+C or select Edit Copy (to copy the text). You can also click on the Cut and Copy buttons on the Standard toolbar.

3. Make the destination document active. Move the insertion point to the location for the new text.

4. Press Ctrl+V, or select Edit Paste, or click on the Paste button on the Standard toolbar.

Seeing Multiple Windows

At times you may want to have two or more open documents visible on the screen at the same time. To do so, select

Window Arrange All. Word displays each open document in its own window in the work area. For example, Figure 27.1 shows three documents displayed in the work area. Note that each document window has its own title bar, displaying the document's name.

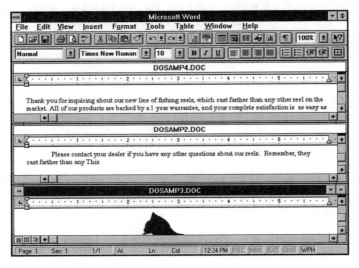

Figure 27.1   Multiple documents displayed with Window Arrange All.

Only one document can be active, or current, at any given time. The current document is indicated by a dark background in the title bar and a dark border. In Figure 27.1, the third document, called DOSAMP3.DOC, is current. To make a different document window current, click anywhere in the window with the mouse. Or you can press Ctrl+F6 one or more times to cycle between windows, or you can select a command from the Window menu as described in Lesson 26.

With multiple document windows displayed, you can control the size and position of each window. If you don't already know how, the appendix, "Microsoft Windows Primer," shows you how to control document windows.

Redisplaying a Document at Full-Screen Size

To clear multiple documents from your screen and return to full-screen display of a single document, follow these steps:

1. Make current the document that you want to display full-screen.

2. Maximize the window by pressing Ctrl+F10 or by clicking on the Maximize button. (The Maximize button is the upward-pointing arrowhead immediately to the right of the window's title bar.)

Saving Multiple Documents

When you are working with multiple documents, you save documents with the File Save and File Save As commands that you learned in Lesson 5. These commands will save only the active document. You can save all open documents with a single command, File Save All.

Closing a Document

You can close an open document once you are finished working with it. To close a document:

1. Make the document active.

2. Select File Close.

3. If the document contains unsaved changes, Word for Windows prompts you to save the document.

4. The document is closed.

In this lesson, you learned how to work with multiple documents. In the next lesson, you'll learn how to use macros to automate your work.

Lesson

28

Saving Time with Macros

In this lesson, you'll learn how to use macros to save time.

What Is a Macro?

A *macro* is a sequence of commands and keystrokes that has been recorded and saved by Word for Windows. You can easily play back a macro at any time, achieving the same result as if you had entered each command and keystroke individually. For example, you could create a macro that:

- Converts an entire document from single-spaced to double-spaced.

- Goes through a document and formats the first word of each paragraph in 18-point italics.

- Saves the document to disk and then prints it in draft mode.

> **Why Macros?**   Macros save time. By recording frequently needed command sequences as macros, you can save time and reduce errors.

   Word for Windows macros are a complex and powerful feature. The basics you'll learn in this lesson will enable you to create many useful macros.

Recording a Macro

The simplest way to create a macro is to enter the keystrokes and commands yourself while Word for Windows records them. The only operations that Word for Windows cannot record are mouse editing actions. That is, a macro cannot record the mouse moving the insertion point or selecting text; you must use the keyboard for these actions while recording a macro. Other mouse actions, such as selecting menu commands or dialog box options, can be recorded in a macro.

To record a macro:

1. Plan the macro. It is often a good idea to try a procedure out before recording it in a macro to ensure that it works the way you want it to.

2. Select Tools Macro to display the Macro dialog box, and then select Record to display the Record Macro dialog box (see Figure 28.1).

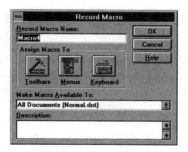

Figure 28.1   The Record Macro dialog box.

3. In the Record Macro Name box, enter a name for the macro. The name should be descriptive of the macro's function. Use any characters except spaces, commas, and periods in the macro name.

4. In the Description box, enter a short description of the macro. Entering a description is optional, but recommended.

5. If the document is based on a template other than NORMAL, you can pull down the Make Macro Available To list and select All Documents (if you want the macro available to all documents) or Documents based On (if you want the macro available only to documents based on the current template).

6. Select OK. Word starts recording the macro. While recording is in progress, Word displays the Macro toolbar in a corner of the document. In addition, the REC indicator is displayed in the status line at the bottom of the screen, and the mouse pointer changes to a recorder symbol to remind you to use the keyboard—not the mouse—to select text and move the insertion point.

7. Execute the actions and commands that you want in the macro.

8. During recording, you can click the Pause button on the Macro toolbar if you want to perform actions that you don't want recorded in the macro. Click Pause again to resume recording.

9. When you are finished, click the Stop button to terminate macro recording and store the macro.

Quick Start Double-click the REC indicator on the status line to start or stop recording a macro.

Playing Back a Macro

You can play back any macro at any time while you're working on a document, as follows:

1. Select Tools Macro. The Macro dialog box appears (see Figure 28.2).

2. Type the name of the macro in the Macro Name box or highlight the name in the list.

3. Select Run. The chosen macro is executed.

Figure 28.2   Choose a macro to run in the Macro dialog box.

Assigning a Shortcut Key to a Macro

If you assign a shortcut key for a macro, you can play the macro back simply by pressing its shortcut key. The shortcut keys are really key combinations; you can select from the following (where *key* is a letter, number, function, or cursor movement key):

Ctrl+*key*

Alt+*key*

Alt+Ctrl+*key*

Alt+Shift+*key*

Ctrl+Shift+*key*

Ctrl+Shift+Alt+*key*

To assign a shortcut key to a macro, follow these steps:

1. Select Tools Customize to display the Customize dialog box.

2. If necessary, click the Keyboard tab to display the keyboard options (see Figure 28.3).

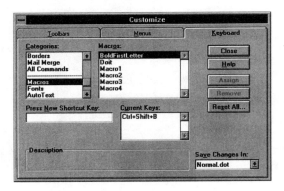

Figure 28.3 Use the Customize dialog box to assign a shortcut key to a macro.

3. Scroll through the Categories list until the Macros entry is highlighted.

4. In the Macros list, highlight the name of the macro to which you want to assign a shortcut key.

5. Click on the Press New Shortcut Key box or press Alt+N.

6. Press the shortcut key combination that you want to assign. Its description is displayed in the Press New ShortCut Key box.

7. Under Current Keys, Word displays the name of the macro or command that the selected shortcut key is assigned to, or Word displays (unassigned) if the shortcut key is not assigned.

8. If the shortcut key is unassigned, select Assign to assign it to the macro. If it is already assigned, press Backspace to delete the shortcut key display, and return to step 6 to try another key combination.

Shortcut Keys   Assign a shortcut key to macros that you will use frequently. To play the macro, simply press the shortcut key while editing the document.

In this lesson you learned how to use macros to automate your work. This is the last lesson in the book. You should now be comfortable enough with Word for Windows to continue learning the program's more advanced features on your own. Good writing!

Appendix

Microsoft Windows Primer

Microsoft Windows is an interface program that makes your computer easier to use by enabling you to select menu items and pictures rather than type commands. Programs that you run under Windows, such as a spreadsheet or word processor, use similar designs for their screen displays, menus, and commands. Before you can use Windows or a Windows program such as the one covered in this book, you must learn some Windows basics.

Starting Microsoft Windows

To start Windows, do the following:

1. At the DOS prompt, type `win`.

2. Press Enter.

The Windows title screen appears for a few moments, and then you see a screen like the one in Figure A.1. This is the Windows Program Manager screen.

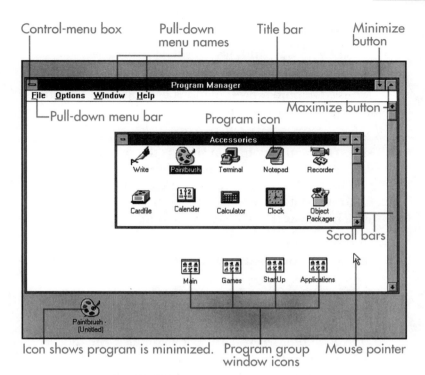

Control-menu box   Pull-down   Title bar   Minimize
                    menu names   button

Pull-down menu bar   Program icon   Maximize button

                                                      Scroll bars

Icon shows program is minimized.   Program group   Mouse pointer
                                    window icons

Figure A.1   The Windows Program Manager screen.

What If It Didn't Work?   You may have to
change to the Windows directory before starting
Windows; to do so, type **CD \WINDOWS** and
press Enter.

Parts of a Windows Screen

As shown in Figure A.1, the Windows screen contains several
unique elements that you won't see in DOS. Here's a brief
summary.

- *Title bar*   Shows the name of the window or program.

- *Program group windows*   Contain program icons that allow you to run programs.

- *Icons*   Graphic representations of programs. To run a program, you select its icon.

- *Minimize and Maximize buttons*   Alter a window's size. The Minimize button shrinks the window to the size of an icon. The Maximize button expands the window to fill the screen. When maximized, a window contains a double-arrow *Restore* button, which returns the window to its original size.

- *Control-menu box*   When selected, pulls down a menu that offers size and location controls for the window.

- *Pull-down menu bar*   Contains a list of the pull-down menus available in the program.

- *Mouse pointer*   If you are using a mouse, the mouse pointer (usually an arrow) appears on-screen. It can be controlled by moving the mouse (discussed in the next section).

- *Scroll bars*   If a window contains more information than can be displayed in the window, a scroll bar appears. *Scroll arrows* on each end of the scroll bar allow you to scroll slowly. The *scroll box* allows you to scroll more quickly.

Using a Mouse

To work most efficiently in Windows, you should use a mouse. You can press mouse buttons and move the mouse in various ways to change the way it acts:

Point means to move the mouse pointer onto the specified item by moving the mouse. The tip of the mouse pointer must be touching the item.

Click on an item means to move the pointer onto the specified item and press the mouse button once. Unless specified otherwise, use the left mouse button.

Double-click on an item means to move the pointer onto the specified item and press and release the mouse button twice quickly.

Drag means to move the mouse pointer onto the specified item, hold down the mouse button, and move the mouse while holding down the button.

Figure A.2 shows how to use the mouse to perform common Windows activities, including running applications and moving and resizing windows.

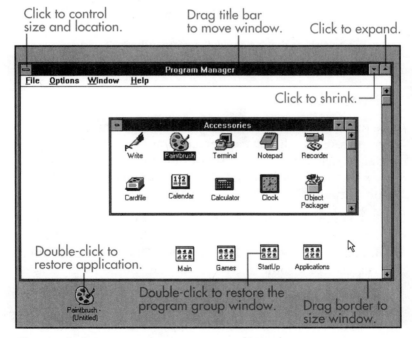

Figure A.2 Use your mouse to control Windows.

Starting a Program

You start programs from the Windows Program Manager screen. This is the screen that is displayed when you first start Windows. If Windows is already running and the Program Manager is not visible, press Alt+Esc one or more times until it is visible.

Once the Program Manager screen is displayed, you start a program by simply double-clicking its icon. If its icon is not visible, it means one of two things:

* The program group window is hidden by other windows. Press Ctrl+F6 one or more times until the window is visible.

* The program group window is not open, but rather is displayed as an icon. Double-click the icon to open the window.

Once the correct program group window is displayed you can double-click the program icon to start the program.

Using Menus

The pull-down menu bar (see Figure A.3) contains various menus from which you can select commands. Each Windows program that you run has a set of pull-down menus; Windows itself has a set too. All Windows menus work in the same manner.

To open a menu, click on its name on the menu bar or by pressing Alt+x, where x is the underlined letter in the menu name, called the selection letter. Once a menu is open, you can select a command from it by clicking on the desired command or by pressing the underlined selection letter.

Shortcut Keys Notice that in Figure A.3, some commands are followed by key names such as Enter (for the **O**pen command) or F8 (for the **C**opy command). These are called *shortcut keys*. You can use these keys to perform these commands without even opening the menu.

Command names   Shortcut keys

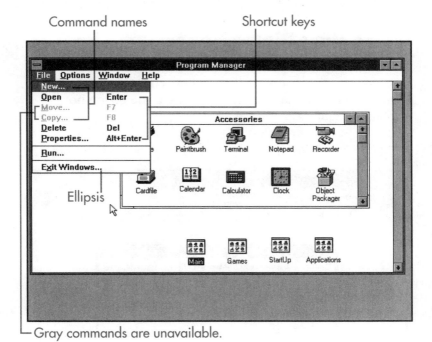

Ellipsis

Gray commands are unavailable.

Figure A.3 A pull-down menu lists various commands you can perform.

Usually, when you select a command, the command is performed immediately. However:

• If the command name is gray (rather than black), the command is unavailable at the moment and you cannot choose it.

- If the command name is followed by an arrow, selecting the command will cause another menu to appear, from which you select another command.

- If the command name is followed by an ellipsis (three dots), selecting it will cause a dialog box to appear. You'll learn about dialog boxes in the next section.

Navigating Dialog Boxes

A dialog box is Windows' way of requesting additional information. For example, if you choose Print from the File menu of the Write application, you'll see the dialog box shown in Figure A.4.

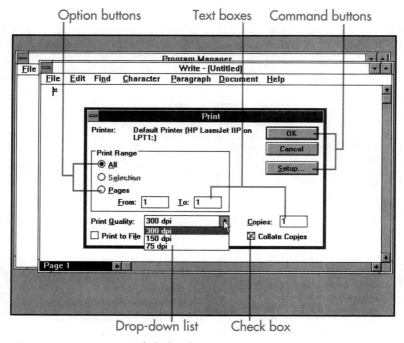

Figure A.4   A typical dialog box.

Each dialog box contains one or more of the following elements:

- *List boxes* display available choices. To activate a list, click inside the list box. If the entire list is not visible, use the scroll bar to view the items in the list. To select an item from the list, click on it.

- *Drop-down lists* are similar to list boxes, but only one item in the list is shown. To see the rest of the items, click on the down arrow to the right of the list box. To select an item from the list, click on it.

- *Text boxes* allow you to type an entry. To activate a text box, click inside it. To edit an existing entry, use the arrow keys to move the cursor and the Del or Backspace keys to delete existing characters, and then type your correction.

- *Check boxes* allow you to select one or more items in a group of options. For example, if you are styling text, you may select Bold and Italic to have the text appear in both bold and italic type. Click on a check box to activate it.

- *Option buttons* are like check boxes, but you can select only one option button in a group. Selecting one button unselects any option that is already selected. Click on an option button to activate it.

- *Command buttons* execute (or cancel) the command once you have made your selections in the dialog box. To press a command button, click on it.

Switching Between Windows

Many times you will have more than one window open at once. Some open windows may be program group windows, while others may be actual programs that are running. To switch among them, you can:

- Pull down the Window menu and choose the window you want to view.

Or

- If a portion of the desired window is visible, click on it.

Controlling a Window

As you saw earlier in this appendix, you can minimize, maximize, and restore windows on your screen. But you can also move them and change their size.

- To move a window, drag its title bar to a different location. (Remember, "drag" means to hold down the left mouse button while you move the mouse.)

- To resize a window, position the mouse pointer on the border of the window until you see a double-headed arrow; then drag the window border to the desired size.

Copying Your Program Diskettes with File Manager

Before you install any new software, you should make a copy of the original diskettes as a safety precaution. Windows' File Manager makes this process easy.

First, start File Manager by double-clicking on the File Manager icon in the Main program group. Then, for each disk you need to copy, follow these steps:

1. Locate a blank disk of the same type as the original disk and label it to match the original. Make sure the disk you select does not contain any data that you want to keep.

2. Place the original disk in your diskette drive (A or B).

3. Open the Disk menu and select Copy Disk. The Copy Disk dialog box appears.

4. Select the drive used in step 2 from the Source In list box.

5. Select the same drive from the Destination In list box. (Don't worry; File Manager will tell you to switch disks at the appropriate time.)

6. Select OK. The Confirm Copy Disk dialog box appears.

7. Select Yes to continue.

8. When instructed to insert the Source diskette, choose OK since you already did this at step 2. The Copying Disk box appears, and the copy process begins.

9. When instructed to insert the target disk, remove the original disk from the drive and insert the blank disk. Then choose OK to continue. The Copying Disk box disappears when the process is complete.

Index